AWESOME
Chemistry Experiments
for Kids

AWESOME CHEMISTRY EXPERIMENTS for Kids

40 STEAM SCIENCE PROJECTS AND WHY THEY WORK

ADRIAN DINGLE

Illustrations by Conor Buckley

ROCKRIDGE PRESS

For general information on our other products and services or to obtain technical support, please contact our Customer Care Department within the United States at (866) 744-2665, or outside the United States at (510) 253-0500.

Rockridge Press publishes its books in a variety of electronic and print formats. Some content that appears in print may not be available in electronic books, and vice versa.

Series Designer: Katy Brown
Interior and Cover Designer: John Clifford
Art Producer: Hannah Dickerson
Editor: Laura Apperson
Production Editor: Chris Gage

Photography © 2021 Emulsion Studio, cover; PeopleImages/iStock.com, back cover (top) and p. 14; fizkes/Shutterstock.com, back cover (center) and p. 98; MelkiNimages/iStock.com, back cover (bottom) and p. X; JGI/Jamie Grill/Blend/Offset.com, p. II. Illustrations © 2021 Conor Buckley, except for Pyty/Shutterstock.com, p. 5.

ISBN: Print 978-1-64876-614-5
eBook 978-1-64739-998-6
R0

All of my writing,
including this book,
is for Olivia and
Matthew.

CONTENTS

PART III

PUTTING IT ALL TOGETHER 99

A NOTE FOR PARENTS

Awesome Chemistry Experiments for Kids features 40 exciting and fun chemistry experiments that will entertain, educate, and maybe even amaze you and your kids.

I've spent the last 31 years teaching and writing about chemistry for kids of all ages. Whether it is guiding students toward success in school or writing award-winning books about the periodic table, chemistry has been my life's work.

Each experiment in this book is designed to be done at home with things that you likely already have on hand or that can be purchased easily and cheaply at a local store or online. We'll go into more detail on how to use the book in chapter 2, but it's important to note now that with the fun comes an important reminder to work safely. When necessary, experiments include specific instructions for safety, but you should always help your children handle chemicals and potential hazards such as heat, glass, and sharp objects with great care. A set of goggles and nitrile gloves for you and your child would be useful to have on hand for many of the projects in this book.

A NOTE FOR KIDS

Welcome to the exciting world of chemistry! In this book, you'll find a bunch of cool experiments for you to try, along with all of the explanations behind the sometimes crazy, smelly, colorful, and often surprising results you'll get.

The experiments will be fun and engaging, but they are also designed to give much more than just a superficial experience. Each one teaches you the chemistry behind the experiment—or the "how" and the "why."

For each project, the instructions should be easy to follow, but sometimes they include words that you may not be familiar with. To help, those unfamiliar words used most (written in bold the first time that they are used) are defined in a glossary at the end of the book (see page 101).

Pay close attention to any safety reminders for each experiment. Don't forget to ask an adult for help. Use common sense, so the fun won't be spoiled by an accident!

THE BASICS

Now, let's get started! Chemists, whom we'll learn more about in just a minute, perform experiments by mixing, heating, stirring, and observing. By doing the 40 experiments in this book, you'll become a chemist yourself.

Before you get into the smells, colors, and messes that you will make, though, it's a good idea for you to understand what chemistry is and what chemists do. In this chapter, you can read a little more about some of the important ideas behind the chemistry adventures you are about to have.

Chapter 1

ALL ABOUT CHEMISTRY

Stuff! **That probably doesn't sound like a very scientific** word to you, but it's a great one to describe what scientists call **matter**. Matter is stuff! Anything that you can see or touch is matter. Matter has two characteristics: it has **volume** (meaning that it takes up space), and it has **mass** (meaning that you can weigh it).

So why does matter *matter* in a book about chemistry? It's simple. Chemistry is the science that studies how one type of matter interacts with other types of matter. That's another way of saying that it deals with interactions that we commonly call *chemical reactions*. Chemistry explores and explains common chemical reactions that we see around us every day. For example, if we want to know why an iron nail rusts, then we need to figure out how the iron interacts with both the water and the oxygen in the air. If we want to know why an apple turns brown when we cut it in half, then we need to find out what the oxygen in the air does to the naturally occurring chemicals in the apple. In fact, you can investigate this in the *Brown Apples* experiment later in the book (page 74)!

ALL ABOUT CHEMISTS

Any person who performs experiments with matter and who studies chemical reactions is called a chemist. You may think of a chemist as being a person in a white lab coat in a laboratory with lots of zany-looking glassware, surrounded by bubbling, colored **liquids**. Some chemists *do* work in places like that, but anyone who studies the way that matter changes is a chemist and is doing chemistry. We are all acting as chemists when we do things like mix ingredients together, heat ingredients to bake bread, or even wash our dirty hands with soap.

THE PERIODIC TABLE

All matter is made up of some combination of the 118 chemical building blocks that we call the **elements**. Some elements you probably know well, but there are other, more exotic ones, such as osmium, bismuth, and vanadium, that you likely won't know as well, like oxygen, iron, and aluminum. Each element has a symbol, and the elements are organized on the periodic table. They are arranged on the table in columns (known as groups) and rows (known as periods), and each element's placement on the table has a specific meaning.

Periodic Table of Elements

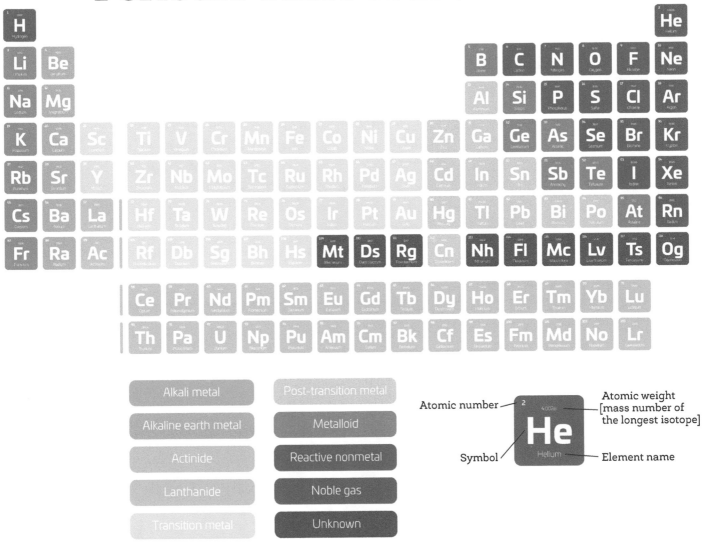

Alkali metal

Alkaline earth metal

Actinide

Lanthanide

Transition metal

Post-transition metal

Metalloid

Reactive nonmetal

Noble gas

Unknown

Atomic number

Atomic weight [mass number of the longest isotope]

Symbol

Element name

THE STATES OF MATTER

A **substance** can exist in one of three forms that we call states of matter. The states are solid, liquid, and **gas**. One substance that you know well is water. Water has the chemical formula H_2O. This tells us that it is made up of hydrogen (H) and oxygen (O), two elements. You know that water is a liquid, but what happens when you freeze or boil water? It changes its state to become a solid or a gas. However, what doesn't change is its chemical composition—it is always H_2O whether it's ice, water, or steam. We can show this by using symbols for states in parentheses: (s), (l), and (g). For example, $H_2O_{(s)}$ = ice (a solid), $H_2O_{(l)}$ = water (a liquid), $H_2O_{(g)}$ = steam (a gas). See the list of possible state changes in the following table. You'll explore these more in the *Chill Out!* experiment (page 18).

Change of State	Name Given to Change
Solid to Liquid	Melting

Liquid to Gas	Boiling

Change of State	Name Given to Change
Gas to Liquid	**Condensation**

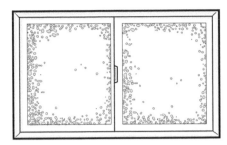

Solid to Gas	**Sublimation**

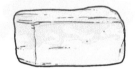

Gas to Solid	Reverse Sublimation or **Deposition**

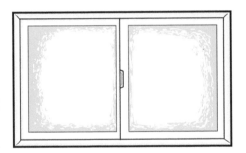

Liquid to Solid	Freezing

THE SCIENTIFIC METHOD

Have you ever asked the question, "Why did that happen?" If you have, then you made an observation. Your curiosity made you wonder about the reason behind something you saw. Scientists do the same thing, and to find answers they apply an idea called the scientific method.

The first step in the scientific method is to think of a hypothesis. A hypothesis is your best guess at an explanation. The hypothesis is often a guess at how one thing affects another. For example, you might say, "Sugar dissolves more easily in hot water than in cold." That's your hypothesis.

The second step is to design and perform an experiment to test your hypothesis. When designing an experiment, it is important to control some variables. For example, you can only do a true study of how water temperature affects **dissolving** sugar if the amount of sugar at different temperatures is kept the same. That way it is a fair experiment.

The next step is to review the results of your experiment. No results are ever wrong if the experiment is executed according to the instructions—they are just the results! If the results don't support your hypothesis, then you might need to change your hypothesis and design a new experiment.

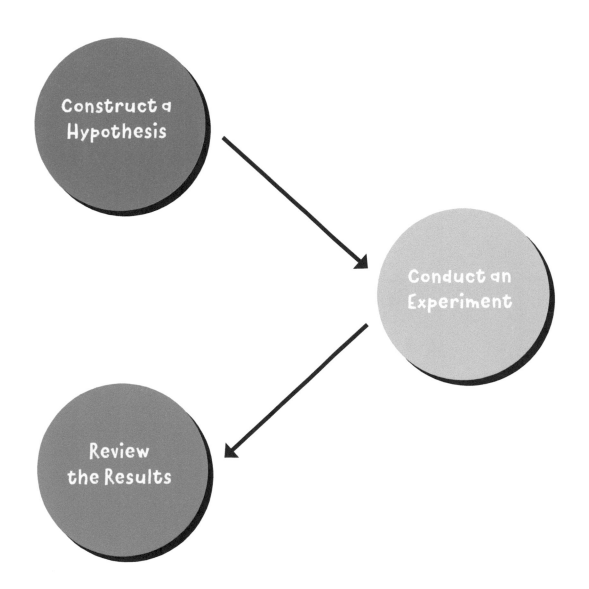

Chapter 2

HOW TO USE THIS BOOK

You can try all of the experiments in the book in any order that you choose. Some experiments may have connections with others, but each one can be conducted as an independent adventure. You should begin by finding an experiment with a title that interests or excites you. Before you start the actual experiment, understand that each one comes with a little guidance to help make things easier and as successful as possible.

The *Mess-O-Meter* rating gives you an idea about what to expect to clean up when you're finished with the experiment. A *minor mess* means there will only be a little bit of cleanup involved, like wiping down a countertop or clearing away some trash, whereas a *medium mess* means the experiment might involve some smells, some foaming or fizzing, or some sticky stuff that might require a little more effort to clean up. But watch out for that *major mess*! That means you might want to try this one outside.

❓ The red question mark identifies the *Big Question*, or the larger idea that you will be investigating. Come back to this after you have performed the experiment to see if you have answered that question.

DOING THE EXPERIMENTS

Before doing an experiment, be prepared! How do you get prepared? Easy! Follow this guide each time that you are ready to try an experiment.

1. Carefully read through the *whole* experiment.
2. Gather the materials.
3. Make sure you understand any safety information and the level of difficulty.
4. Think about the experiment in terms of what you will need to finish it, such as how much space you will need or if you'll need the help of an adult.
5. Follow the step-by-step instructions carefully.

When you have completed the experiment, read *The Hows and Whys* section. There you'll find an explanation of the chemistry involved, and that will help you understand your observations and results. This is where the real chemistry learning is found! In the *Now Try This!* section, you will find ideas on how to push the experiment—and your knowledge—further. Any materials you need that are different from the main experiment will be noted in the experiment's *Materials* section.

When you take note of the results, be prepared to be surprised! Even if things don't work out as you might expect, don't worry. The learning never stops. Keep going, try again, perhaps with a slightly different approach, and, above all else, have fun!

DO'S AND DON'TS

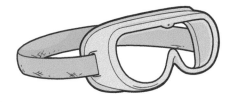

In many experiments you'll see some instructions about safety that you should follow carefully. In addition to the specific instructions, always think about how to become a better chemist. Here are some do's and don'ts that will help make you the best chemist you can be.

DO:

1. Follow instructions carefully, especially any that tell you about safety, like wearing goggles, wearing gloves, or getting an adult to help.
2. Keep your work area tidy by cleaning up any spills as soon as they happen.
3. Wash your hands thoroughly before and after you have completed an experiment.

DON'T:

1. Don't play around when performing experiments. It could be dangerous and mess up your experiment and its results. It's important to focus on the experiment you are doing.
2. Don't mix chemicals together randomly. Sometimes an unpleasant or even dangerous reaction can occur that you weren't expecting.

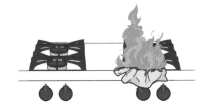

Part II

THE EXPERIMENTS

Okay, are you ready to have some chemistry fun? Good, because here we go!

In this part, you'll find 40 super-cool experiments that will spark your interest in chemistry. Again, each one comes with a set of instructions that you should follow closely. Remember to read through each experiment carefully before you start, and plan wisely, especially when it comes to safety precautions.

The experiments have been tested to make sure that they work, so if you run into trouble, go back and read the instructions carefully once more, and try again. Don't forget to look closely; make a note of what you see, hear, or smell; and be ready for some interesting results. Happy experimenting!

CRYSTAL BALL

DIFFICULTY: MEDIUM

TIME: 20 MINUTES

MESS-O-METER:

MEDIUM MESS

MATERIALS

- Measuring cups
- A large mixing bowl
- Warm water
- A smaller bowl
- ¼ cup dish soap
- A kitchen towel
- Gloves
- Dry ice
- A narrow piece of cotton material that is as long as the width of the large bowl (like a T-shirt collar)
- A fork (Now Try This!)

 What are the different states of matter, and how can they be changed from one to another?

 Caution: Dry ice needs to be handled with gloves and adult supervision.

THE STEPS

1. Fill the large bowl with warm water until it is 3-4 cm full.

2. In the separate, smaller bowl, make a very soapy **solution** using water and the dish soap.

3. Using a kitchen towel, rub some of the soapy solution all the way around the rim of the large bowl.

4. Using protective gloves, place several pieces of dry ice into the large bowl with the warm water.

5. Take the cotton material, and holding the ends, dip it into the soapy solution to get it nice and wet.

6. Hold the ends of the now soapy cotton material so it is stretched out to its full length. Slowly drag it across the top of the large bowl to leave a sealed, thin film of soap across the top of the whole bowl. This can be a little fiddly, so you may need to try a few times!

Observations: Watch the dry ice carefully as it sits in the warm water under the soap layer. What do you see?

The Hows and Whys: Dry ice is solid carbon dioxide that will produce gaseous CO_2 (the chemical formula for carbon dioxide) when it warms up. Trapping the carbon dioxide gas inside the soapy bubble allows the bubble to inflate. Solid carbon dioxide undergoes a process called sublimation as it warms up. Sublimation is when a solid turns directly into a gas without forming a liquid. When substances change from solids to liquids or gases and back again, they are undergoing a change of state (see the section on states of matter on page 6).

Now Try This! When the bubble is inflated, poke it with a fork!

STEAM CONNECTION: Scientists are seeking ways to remove carbon dioxide from the atmosphere since it is a harmful greenhouse gas. Greenhouse gases act like blankets around the earth and its atmosphere, and have the effect of raising the temperature of our environment.

CHILL OUT!

DIFFICULTY: EASY

TIME: 15 MINUTES

MESS-O-METER: MINOR MESS

MATERIALS

- Water
- An empty soda can
- A small bowl
- Ice
- A source of heat (like a griddle or frying pan on the stove top)
- Oven mitts
- Metal tongs

 What happens when you quickly cool a gas?

 Caution: Ask an adult for help with this one. It involves a lot of very hot parts.

THE STEPS

1. Pour just enough water into the empty soda can to cover the bottom about 1 cm deep.

2. Fill the bowl three-fourths full of cold water and ice cubes.

3. Place the soda can onto your prepared heat source and wait for the water in the can to boil.

4. After a couple of minutes, you will see steam coming out of the can. Have an adult wearing oven mitts and using tongs pick up the can and quickly plunge it, open-end first, into the ice water.

Observations: As the can heats up, watch the opening at the top from a safe distance. What do you see?

The Hows and Whys: When the water is heated, it boils and turns into a gas called steam. This is an example of a change of state from liquid to gas. (See the states of matter section on page 6.) The hot steam pushes the air out of the can, and the can fills with steam. The steam creates pressure inside the can. When the can comes into contact with the ice-cold water, the steam condenses, turns back into water, and the pressure in the can drops. When this happens, the air pressure outside of the can is greater than the pressure inside the can, and the can is crushed from the outside.

Now Try This! Try the same experiment, this time putting cold water without ice in the bowl, then again using warm water instead of ice water. Do you see any differences between using ice-cold water, just cold water, or warm water?

STEAM CONNECTION: Gases take up lots of space, so to transport them in smaller containers, technology is used to convert them to liquids that are more compact.

WATER SPLITTER

DIFFICULTY: MEDIUM, BUT
YOU'LL NEED 2 PAIRS
OF HANDS
TIME: 30 MINUTES
MESS-O-METER: MINOR MESS

 What is water made of?

 Caution: You'll be using some matches and sharp thumbtacks. Get an adult to help.

MATERIALS

- Measuring spoons
- 2 thumbtacks
- A small, clear 8-ounce plastic cup
- Water
- 2 teaspoons table salt
- A 9V battery
- 2 test tubes or 2-ounce squeeze bottles (Often, food coloring comes in bottles like this.)
- Matches (Now Try This!)

THE STEPS

1. Press the thumbtacks into the bottom of the clear plastic cup. Make sure they are not touching each other, but close enough together so that the battery terminals can touch both of them.

2. Fill the cup three-fourths full of water.

3. Stir in the table salt until it is completely dissolved.

4. Touch the battery terminals to the thumbtacks and hold the battery there.

5. After 30 seconds, hold the empty squeeze bottles underwater until they each fill with water. Don't stop holding the battery—this is why you need a second pair of hands!

6. Place 1 bottle over 1 thumbtack, and the other bottle over the other thumbtack, holding in place if necessary. Wait until each bottle fills with gas.

Observations: Make a careful note about the amounts of gas that are being produced at each battery terminal. Which terminal is producing more gas?

The Hows and Whys: Water has the chemical formula H_2O. That means the **molecule** is made up of 2 hydrogen **atoms** and 1 oxygen atom. Because of this, you can use electricity to split it into two gases, hydrogen and oxygen. The electricity provides the energy to split the water molecules apart.

Now Try This! Once you have filled each of the bottles with gas (in step 5), you can test for the type of gases in each one. Remove the bottle that was at the negative terminal of the battery, and quickly hold a lighted match close to the open end. Hydrogen gas explodes and will make a squeaky *pop* sound. You can test the gas produced at the positive terminal by bringing a glowing splint close to oxygen. A *glowing splint* is a thin piece of wood (in this case, a match) that has been lit, then blown out so that it is still glowing red hot but not burning. It should relight.

STEAM CONNECTION: Chemical **compounds** that are usually quite stable, like water, can be broken apart into their basic elements with electricity. This process is called electrolysis. The electrolysis of sea water produces three important chemicals: chlorine, hydrogen, and sodium hydroxide. Chlorine is used as a disinfectant, hydrogen is used in making fertilizers, and sodium hydroxide is used to make soap.

EVAPORATION RACE

MATERIALS

- Measuring cups
- Room-temperature water
- Hot water
- 2 plastic zipper-seal sandwich bags
- 2 unbleached (brown) coffee filters
- An eyedropper
- Rubbing alcohol (Now Try This!)
- Acetone (Now Try This!)

 Does temperature affect how quickly water evaporates?

 Cautions: None

THE STEPS

1. Pour ½ cup of room-temperature water into 1 sandwich bag and ½ cup of hot water into the other. Squeeze all the air out of the bags, and zip them up to seal them tight.

2. Cut out 2 (10-cm) squares out of the brown coffee filters.

3. Using the eyedropper, put 1 drop of room-temperature water in the center of each square of the coffee filters.

4. Place 1 of the coffee filter squares on the room-temperature water bag, and the other on the hot water bag.

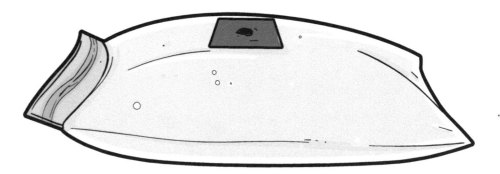

5. After 5 minutes, look at the coffee filters. Look again after another 5 minutes. Continue to check them every 5 minutes for about 30 minutes in total.

Observations: What do you notice about the two filters and the size of the water spot?

The Hows and Whys: Evaporation is a change of state where a liquid turns into a gas. For evaporation to take place, the molecules need to gain energy so that they can break apart from one another and change from a liquid to a gas. The forces that hold one molecule to another are called intermolecular forces. When these attractions are strong, more energy is needed to break them apart. In this experiment, the hot water bag will give more energy to the water on the coffee filter than the room-temperature bag. The extra energy allows the water molecules to break apart from one another and form a gas.

Now Try This! Repeat the experiment using rubbing alcohol and acetone on the coffee filters instead of water. What do you notice about the speed of evaporation?

STEAM CONNECTION: Stepping out of the shower will make you feel cold. As the water molecules on your skin evaporate and turn into a gas, they absorb energy from your body. As you lose energy, your body feels cold!

BALLOON CONDITIONS

MATERIALS

- 2 balloons
- A fabric measuring tape, or a piece of string and a ruler
- A refrigerator
- A 20 to 30 mL Luer lock syringe, with no needle (Now Try This!)
- A mini marshmallow (Now Try This!)

 How do gases behave when we change the outside conditions?

 Cautions: None

THE STEPS

1. Blow up a balloon and tie the end.

2. Wrap a measuring tape or a piece of string around the widest part of the balloon to measure the circumference of the balloon. If you use a piece of string, you can then measure the length of the string with a regular ruler.

3. Blow up another balloon, and tie the end, making the second balloon as close to exactly the same size as the first one. Measure its circumference using the same method as you did in step 2.

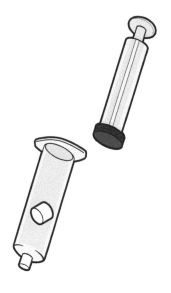

4. Place 1 of the balloons in the fridge.

5. After 45 minutes, take the cold balloon out of the fridge, and measure the circumference of each balloon again.

Observations: Record any changes in size.

> **The Hows and Whys:** Cooling the **particles** in a gas means that they move more slowly and get closer together. They take up less space and the cold balloon will shrink to a smaller size (a smaller volume).

Now Try This! To investigate how a gas acts when the pressure (instead of the temperature) changes, try this experiment. Using a 20 to 30 mL plastic Luer lock syringe with no needle, remove the plunger and place a mini marshmallow inside. Put the plunger back into the syringe so it is about two-thirds of the way in. Cap the syringe so that it is sealed tightly. Now pull the plunger out and then push the plunger back in, watching the marshmallow all the time.

STEAM CONNECTION: Boyle's law says that whatever pressure does, volume does the opposite. For example, if pressure decreases, volume increases. When you go to the doctor to get a shot, the syringe works using Boyle's law. When the plunger is pulled out, the volume increases inside the syringe, and the pressure drops. The liquid that is being drawn into the syringe rushes in to fill the low-pressure area.

POTATO GAS

MATERIALS

- A knife
- A large potato
- A freezer
- 3 (8-ounce) glasses
- 12 ounces
  3% hydrogen peroxide

 What affects the speed of a chemical reaction?

 Caution: Sharp knives should only be handled with adult supervision.

THE STEPS

1. Using the knife, peel and cut off the ends of the potato to make it into a single, cylindrical block.

2. Cut the potato block into 3 equal-size smaller blocks. Making the blocks as similar to each other as possible makes the experiment a fair test.

3. Keep 2 potato blocks at room temperature for 45 minutes and put the third into a freezer for the same amount of time.

4. Ask an adult to help you cut 1 of the room-temperature blocks into several smaller pieces, each piece about the size of a pea.

5. Fill all 3 glasses halfway with the hydrogen peroxide. Make sure there is enough for the potatoes to be completely covered by liquid when added.

6. Add 1 type of potato (cold, room temperature, or chopped) to each glass. Watch carefully.

Observations: What do you notice about how fast the bubbles are being produced in each glass?

The Hows and Whys: The chemical reaction that is happening is the breakdown of hydrogen peroxide into water and oxygen gas. The oxygen gas bubbles are what you see. An **enzyme** in the potato called catalase makes the reaction happen. Many different things affect the speed of a chemical reaction. Temperature and particle size are two of those things. Higher temperatures and smaller particles make reactions go faster.

Now Try This! Try boiling a potato in water for about 15 minutes. Use that in the experiment. You can also try cutting your potato pieces into different sizes and shapes.

STEAM CONNECTION: Surface area makes a big difference in food chemistry. Since powdered sugar is sugar in very fine pieces, it will dissolve faster than sugar cubes.

RELEASE THE GAS!

DIFFICULTY: EASY
TIME: 15 MINUTES
MESS-O-METER: MINOR MESS

MATERIALS

- 3 clear cups
- Clear soda (like 7 Up or Sprite)
- M&Ms candy
- Skittles candy
- Mentos candy
- Diet soda (Now Try This!)

 How does candy react with soda?

 Cautions: **None**

THE STEPS

1. Fill each cup about half full of soda.

2. Place an M&M in the first cup, a Skittle in the second, and a Mentos in the third.

3. Watch the 3 cups carefully and make a note of your observations.

Observations: Is there any difference in how fast, or how many, bubbles are released by each type of candy?

The soda is a sugary solution with lots and lots of carbon dioxide gas dissolved in it to make it fizzy. When the carbon dioxide has a surface to collect on, the tiny gas molecules will come together to make large bubbles of carbon dioxide.

Now Try This! Try the classic Mentos and diet soda experiment by dropping a Mentos into a bottle of diet soda. Note that it's best to use *diet* soda, not regular soda, since the cleanup will be less sticky! Do this one outside, because it will make a really big mess! Also, try scratching the Mentos with a fork or a wire brush to make the surface rougher, and repeat the experiment. What do you notice?

STEAM CONNECTION: The different types of candy all appear to have smooth surfaces, but at the microscopic level, the surfaces are very uneven and bumpy. The uneven surface allows the carbon dioxide gas molecules to collect and gather together in the tiny holes and crevices until they make a bubble large enough for you to see. The bubbles then rise up through the soda. These tiny collection sites are called **nucleation sites**. Very sensitive devices called scanning electron microscopes (SEMs) can be used to examine these nucleation sites that are otherwise impossible to see with the naked eye.

DENSITY TOWER

DIFFICULTY: MEDIUM
TIME: 30 MINUTES
MESS-O-METER:
MEDIUM MESS

MATERIALS

- Honey
- Corn syrup
- Milk
- Dish soap
- Water
- Vegetable oil
- Rubbing alcohol
- 7 small disposable plastic cups with spouts for pouring
- Food coloring
- A tall glass
- A funnel with a long spout

 What is **density**, and how does it affect the behavior of liquids?

Caution: Rubbing alcohol should be handled with adult supervision in a well-ventilated room.

THE STEPS

1. Pour small samples of honey, corn syrup, milk, dish soap, water, vegetable oil, and rubbing alcohol into separate containers. Any container will do, but small, plastic measuring cups with spouts are great for this experiment.

2. Add different food colorings to the liquids. You can use whatever colors you'd like, but in this experiment, honey is red, corn syrup is orange, milk is yellow, dish soap is green, water is blue, vegetable oil is purple, and rubbing alcohol is pink. Not all of the liquids will mix with the food coloring well, so experiment with that, too!

3. Pour the honey carefully into the tall glass, trying to not get any on the sides.

4. Then, also very carefully, add the corn syrup as a second layer on top of the honey. By pouring slowly, you should be able to stop the 2 layers from mixing. Allow the 2 layers to settle.

5. Add the milk as the next layer by pouring it slowly into the funnel, with the spout just above the corn syrup layer. Rinse out the funnel when you're done.

6. Next, add layers of the dish soap, water, vegetable oil, and finally, rubbing alcohol in the same way as the milk, rinsing out the funnel in between each layer.

Observations: Which liquids mix well with the food coloring and which ones do not? Watch how the layers of liquid settle on top of one another. What do you notice?

The Hows and Whys: Density measures how much material is collected in a given space. Mathematically, it is calculated by dividing the mass of an object by its volume. Liquids with high densities have lots of material in a small space and have a high density. They will sink below other liquids with lower densities.

Now Try This! Cut cubes of several different cheeses into the size of dice. Make sure that the pieces are as close to the same size as possible. Weigh each piece on a digital kitchen scale. Which cheese has the highest density, or weighs the most?

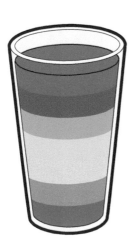

STEAM CONNECTION: One of the most dense metals is lead, which was used in fishing weights. We now know that lead is a very toxic substance to humans, fish, and other wildlife, so like lead-based paints, lead weights have been phased out.

WATER STACKING

DIFFICULTY: MEDIUM
TIME: 30 MINUTES
MESS-O-METER: MINOR MESS

MATERIALS

- Red and blue food coloring
- 4 (12-ounce) clear plastic containers
- 24 ounces cold water
- 24 ounces hot water
- 2 playing cards

 How is density affected by temperature?

 Caution: Hot water can burn. Ask an adult for help.

THE STEPS

1. Put 2 or 3 drops of red food coloring into 2 of the glass bottles. Then fill them to the brim with the hot water.

2. Take the other 2 bottles and fill them in the same way as in step 1, but this time, use blue food coloring and cold water.

3. Slide 1 playing card over the top of 1 of the bottles with red, hot water, making a seal. Do the same with another playing card on 1 of the bottles with blue, cold water.

4. Carefully hold the playing card in place, turn the red, hot water bottle upside down, and balance it on top of the uncovered blue, cold water bottle. Do the same with the other blue, cold water bottle, placing it on top of the other uncovered red, hot water bottle. You should now have a pair of stacked water bottles, each with a playing card separating the two bottles. One will have a red, hot water bottle on top, and the other will have a blue, cold water bottle on top.

5. Holding the top bottle steady, gently slide the playing card out from between the bottles, keeping one bottle stacked on top of the other. Repeat for the other pair of stacked bottles.

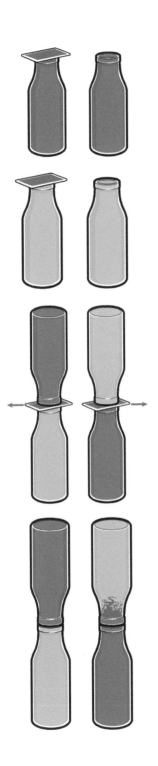

Observations: When the cards are removed, watch the colors in the bottles carefully. What do you notice about the difference between the two stacks?

The Hows and Whys: This experiment is all about the how the density of water changes with temperature. A more dense substance is heavier than the same amount of a less dense substance. Hot water is less dense than cold water. When the hot water is placed on top of the cold water, the more dense cold water stays at the bottom, and the less dense hot water stays at the top. When the cold water is on top, the less dense warm water rises into the top bottle and the cold water sinks into the bottom bottle.

Now Try This! Rubbing alcohol is less dense than water. Try the experiment again using rubbing alcohol in place of the hot water. What happens?

STEAM CONNECTION: Convection currents, when warm and cold liquids and gases rise and fall according to their densities, occur in the oceans and the atmosphere. These currents affect the weather, often causing windy conditions. As air gets heated by the sun it will rise, leaving behind an area of low pressure. Air will move from an area of high pressure to the low-pressure area, and the movement of air in this way is what we experience as wind.

HOW SWEET IT IS

DIFFICULTY: EASY

TIME: 30 MINUTES

MESS-O-METER: MINOR MESS

MATERIALS

- Measuring spoons
- Measuring cups
- A large bucket
- Water
- 2 small cups
- 4 teaspoons sugar
- A spoon
- 2 packets artificial sweetener (the kind that comes in a pink packet)
- 2 (2-ounce) plastic bottles with lids
- 1 can regular soda (Now Try This!)
- 1 can diet soda (same brand as the regular soda) (Now Try This!)

 How is sugar different from artificial sugar?

 Cautions: None

THE STEPS

1. Fill the bucket three-fourths full with water.

2. In 1 of the cups, dissolve the sugar in about ¼ cup of water.

3. In the other cup, dissolve the artificial sweetener in about ¼ cup of water.

4. Fill 1 of the small, plastic bottles with the sugar solution.

5. Fill the other small plastic bottle with the sweetener solution.

6. Cap the bottles firmly.

7. Drop the 2 sealed bottles into the bucket.

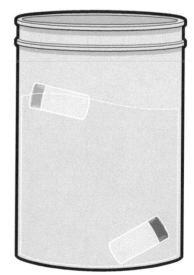

Observations: Watch what each small bottle does in the bucket. Does it float or sink?

The Hows and Whys: Since the sugar solution is much denser than the sweetener solution, the bottle will sink in the water.

Now Try This! Fill the bucket about three-fourths full of water again. Place your unopened cans of diet and regular soda in the water. Make sure no air is trapped in the curve in the bottom of the cans. What do you notice? You can also repeat the original experiment with blue and yellow packet artificial sweeteners. Is there a difference?

STEAM CONNECTION: Acrylic paints of different colors tend to have different densities. For example, white paint tends to be less dense than black paint. Higher density paints will sink below lower density paints, so artists can pour less dense paints on top of more dense paints to create special effects in their art.

COLD SODA

 How can we quickly freeze soda?

 Caution: Very cold water and ice mixtures can be painful to touch.

MATERIALS

- Measuring cups
- 1 liter plastic bottle club soda
- Water
- 5 cups crushed ice
- Rock salt or table salt
- A large bucket
- A spoon
- A thermometer that reads down to -4°F
- 2 saucepans (Now Try This!)

THE STEPS

1. Put a bottle of club soda in the fridge (not the freezer!) overnight (12 hours).

2. The next day, make an ice bath with water, the crushed ice, and rock salt in the large bucket. Half fill the bucket with ice. Fill the remainder of the bucket almost to the top with cold water. Add one cup of salt. Stir well. Add more salt, one tablespoon at a time, to lower the temperature further if necessary.

3. Place the club soda bottle in the ice bath so it is completely underwater.

4. Use the thermometer to watch the temperature of the ice bath. You want to cool the bottle down to about 17°F and to have it sit at that temperature for a few minutes. But don't allow the temperature to drop below 14°F. Alternatively, if the ice is not cold enough, use another cup of rock salt.

5. Once the bottle is cold enough and reaches 17°F, remove it from the ice bath.

6. Holding the bottle upright, unscrew the cap and watch!

Observations: What do you notice about the temperature of the ice bath as you stir in step 2? What happened to the bottle when you unscrewed the cap?

The Hows and Whys: The salt lowers the **freezing point** of the ice bath, taking it below the usual freezing point of pure water of 32°F. The very cold ice bath allows the club soda to get really cold. The carbon dioxide gas that is dissolved in the club soda lowers the freezing point of the bottle's contents. When you open the cap of the bottle and the carbon dioxide escapes, the freezing point of the club soda goes up from about 14°F to the temperature that you reached in the ice bath. When that happens, boom! It freezes!

Now Try This! You can change the **boiling point** of water by adding some salt. Test this out by filling 2 saucepans with 2 cups water each. Add a lot of salt to one pan. Heat the plain water first and use a thermometer to note the temperature when you first start to see bubbles. Repeat with the salted water and compare the two temperatures.

STEAM CONNECTION: The antifreeze used in cars is a mixture of an alcohol and water, which freezes well below the normal freezing point of pure water, 0°C, preventing the car's fluids from turning into a solid!

SPEEDY MELT

DIFFICULTY: EASY
TIME: 30 MINUTES
MESS-O-METER: MINOR MESS

MATERIALS

- Measuring spoons
- 4 ice cubes
- 4 small plates
- ¼ teaspoon salt
- ¼ teaspoon sand
- ¼ teaspoon sugar

 Can we control the speed of melting ice?

 Cautions: None

THE STEPS

1. Pick out 4 ice cubes that are as similar in size and shape as possible. By keeping the ice cubes as close to identical as you can, you are making the experiment a fair test (page 8).

2. Place 1 ice cube in the center of each plate.

3. Carefully sprinkle the salt onto the top of the first cube. Try to keep as much of the salt as possible on top of the cube.

4. Repeat step 3 with the sand instead of salt on the second cube, then the sugar instead of salt on the third cube. Leave the fourth ice cube untouched.

5. Leave the cubes out in the open for about 1 hour, checking on them every 5-10 minutes.

Observations: Watch each cube carefully and see if you can tell which one is melting faster each time you check on them.

The Hows and Whys: Adding salt to the cubes will cause them to melt faster than a regular ice cube. This is called freezing point depression. Freezing point depression is a colligative property. You can learn more about colligative properties by doing the *Cold Soda* experiment (page 36). You can learn more about **ions** in the *Doughy Circuits* experiment (page 70).

Now Try This! Repeat the experiment with more salt, sand, and sugar to see if that makes a difference. You can get some quantitative data (results that include numbers) by timing how long it takes for each ice cube to melt or by measuring the height of the cubes every 10 minutes.

STEAM CONNECTION: The particles of salt prevent the easy formation of the solid water structure, so the H_2O has to be colder before it can form the solid, or it has to be colder before it can freeze. This is why salt is spread on roads in the winter—to help keep the roads from freezing. In ice-cream making, salt is combined with ice to make it very cold, which helps freeze the cream. It's possible to lower the freezing point of water by many degrees using this method.

CRYSTAL SOLUTIONS

DIFFICULTY: MEDIUM

TIME: 3 HOURS

MESS-O-METER:
MEDIUM MESS

MATERIALS

- ➔ Measuring cups
- ➔ Measuring spoons
- ➔ 6 cups distilled white vinegar
- ➔ A saucepan
- ➔ 5 tablespoons baking soda
- ➔ A stove
- ➔ A large glass bowl
- ➔ Aluminum foil

? How do stalagmites form?

! Caution: You'll be using the stove, so you'll need an adult's help.

THE STEPS

1. Pour the vinegar into the saucepan, and add the baking soda, 1 tablespoon at a time. Add slowly to prevent it from foaming over.

2. Heat the solution on the stove over low to medium heat for about 1 hour. Keep an eye on the liquid, and heat until the volume of liquid has reduced by about 90 percent. When you see crystals form on the surface of the liquid, most of the water will have evaporated and it's time to take it off the heat.

3. Pour the resulting solution into the glass bowl, cover it with aluminum foil, and allow it to cool down slowly to room temperature. Slow cooling is best; this may take up to an hour.

4. There will be a few crystals left in the saucepan after you have poured the liquid out. Scrape as many of the white crystals from the inside of the saucepan as you can and set them aside.

5. Once the solution in the bowl has cooled, stick your index finger into the crystals from the saucepan, making sure that some crystals stick to the end of your finger.

6. When you are ready, place your finger with the crystals into the cooled solution in the bowl.

Observations: Look closely at the formation of the crystals. Can you describe their shape? What else do you notice as the crystals form around your finger in the bowl?

The Hows and Whys: The reaction between the vinegar and baking soda releases lots of carbon dioxide gas, and that's the fizzing that you see. The reaction also forms a solution of the chemical called sodium acetate. Boiling off most of the water makes the sodium acetate solution have a lot of sodium acetate for a very small amount of water. When you bring the crystals from your finger into the solution, the sodium acetate starts to rapidly crystalize on the surface of the crystals on your finger.

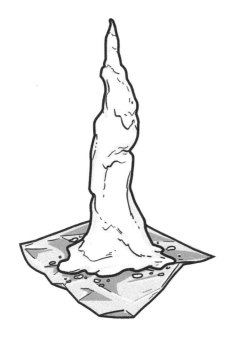

Now Try This! Instead of using your finger, put a small stack of crystals from the saucepan onto a piece of aluminum foil. Very slowly and very carefully pour the cool solution onto them. See if you can make a hot ice stalagmite!

STEAM CONNECTION: A stalagmite is a rock formation that rises from the floor of a cave. Drippings from the ceiling of the cave build up on top of one another to form a column. Stalagmites are often made from calcium compounds such as calcium carbonate.

DIFFICULTY: EASY
TIME: 30 MINUTES TO PREPARE AND THEN LEAVE OVERNIGHT
MESS-O-METER: MEDIUM MESS

MATERIALS

- Measuring spoons
- Measuring cups
- Pipe cleaners
- Scissors
- A medium Mason jar
- A medium saucepan
- 3 cups water
- A source of heat, such as a stove
- 9–12 tablespoons borax powder
- Food coloring (optional)
- String
- A pencil

 How do crystals form?

Caution: You'll be using the stove, so you'll need an adult's help.

THE STEPS

1. Out of the pipe cleaners, form a shape of any kind that you like (stars, snowflakes, 3D cubes, or even animal shapes are all popular choices). You can bend them or cut them however you like; just make sure that the final shape is small enough to fit into the Mason jar and still be removed easily.

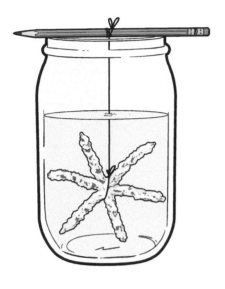

2. In the saucepan, heat the water over medium-high heat. When the water is close to boiling (tiny bubbles will start forming), add 9 tablespoons of borax powder to start. Stir the solution really well. Add the remaining 3 tablespoons of borax one by one until you can't dissolve any more and there is a small amount of undissolved borax at the bottom of the saucepan. Note that your solution shouldn't be cloudy, though. This is now your saturated solution. Remove from the heat.

3. Pour the borax solution into the Mason jar so it is about three-fourths filled. Add a few drops of food coloring if you want colored crystals.

4. Tie a string to a pencil and then attach the string to your pipe-cleaner shape. Rest the pencil on the mouth of the jar so the pipe-cleaner shape is completely covered in solution but not touching the bottom of the jar.

5. Set the jar aside and check on it every hour until you go to bed. Then, leave it overnight. Don't touch the jar while it is cooling!

Observations: Once the jar has been set up, come back to it to see if you can see the crystals beginning to form. Look to see if you can make out the crystals' shape.

The Hows and Whys: The saturated solution contains lots and lots of dissolved borax. By adding the pipe-cleaner shape, you give the crystals a surface where they can grow as the solution cools. The crystals keep growing on top of one another to build the shape.

CONTINUED

Now Try This! Try to make an even bigger crystal by taking the first one you made and leaving it overnight again in a fresh borax solution. How big can you make the crystals?

STEAM CONNECTION: Did you know that snowflakes are ice crystals? Crystals grow in a repeating pattern called a unit cell. The unit cell has a distinct shape that is too small to see without a microscope, but billions of them grow on top of one another in exactly the same shape and create the overall repeating pattern called the crystal lattice. Eventually, they get big enough for you to see. Lots of borax will dissolve in the water, and some may also form what is called a suspension, where it remains as a solid with very tiny particles. Either way, there is a lot of borax in the solution that you make in this experiment. As the solution cools, the water can hold less and less of the borax. Anywhere that offers a surface for the crystals to start to grow on top of one another is called a nucleation site. For more information on nucleation sites, do the *Release the Gas!* experiment (page 28).

GRASS CHROMATOGRAPHY

MATERIALS

- Freshly cut grass
- Scissors
- #4 coffee filter (white)
- A pencil
- A ruler
- A quarter
- Nail polish remover
- Rubbing alcohol
- A tall glass
- A small saucer or plate

 Can we see the chemicals in grass?

 Caution: The substances in this project should be handled with supervision. They can be stinky, so do this experiment outside or in a well-ventilated room.

THE STEPS

1. Gather a few blades of grass.

2. Using scissors, trim the coffee filter into a rectangle that is narrow enough to fit inside the glass and long enough to reach the bottom of the container, but not bowing when the glass is covered. Using a pencil and ruler, draw a line across the paper, about 3 cm from the bottom.

CONTINUED

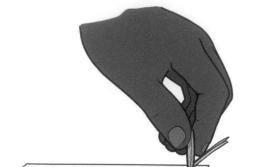

3. Place the grass on the middle of the pencil line on the coffee filter. Use the edge of a quarter to press down hard on the grass so that a dark green spot is left on the paper. Press down several times to get a really dark spot. Set the grass aside.

4. Mix equal amounts of nail polish remover and rubbing alcohol to create a **solvent**. Pour the solvent into the tall glass so that it's 1 cm deep.

5. Carefully stand the filter paper in the glass, with the grass spot at the bottom, making sure to keep the spot above the level of the solvent mixture.

6. Place the small saucer or plate over the top of the glass and wait.

7. After about 20 minutes, the solvent will have traveled most of the way up the paper. Remove the paper from the glass and let it dry.

Observations: What color is the grass spot now that the experiment is over? How does that color compare to the rest of the filter paper?

The Hows and Whys: Grass has a mixture of different chemicals in it, such as chlorophyll and carotene. The molecules in the paper attract some of those chemicals, while the solvent attracts others. The molecules attracted to the solvent travel furthest up the paper, those attracted to the paper travel less far. As a result, the chemicals separate, and you can tell what chemicals are in the mixture by comparing how far each one travels to known values. You can also tell how many chemicals are in the mixture.

Now Try This! Repeat the experiment using colored flower petals or leaves instead of grass to see how many different chemicals are in those samples. You can also investigate using different solvent mixtures like water, mineral spirits, or denatured alcohol, which you can find at your local hardware store.

STEAM CONNECTION: Separating mixtures in a substance, such as grass, in this way is an important chemistry technique called chromatography. For example, scientists who work with the police in forensics can determine if blood samples contain certain poisons by separating them out using chromatography.

SPICY INDICATORS

DIFFICULTY: EASY
TIME: 30 MINUTES
MESS-O-METER: MINOR MESS

MATERIALS

- Measuring spoons
- Measuring cups
- A large bowl
- ½ teaspoon powdered turmeric
- ½ cup rubbing alcohol
- 6 (2-ounce) glass bowls or other small containers (such as egg cups)
- ¼ teaspoon baking soda
- Water
- ¼ teaspoon lemon juice
- ¼ teaspoon distilled white vinegar
- ¼ teaspoon milk
- ¼ teaspoon colorless window cleaner solution
- ¼ teaspoon ammonia
- An eyedropper

 Can a common spice tell you if a substance is an **acid** or a **base**?

 Caution: Ammonia solution should be handled with gloves and goggles.

THE STEPS

1. In the large bowl, combine the turmeric powder and rubbing alcohol, and mix well. This is your **indicator** solution.

2. In 1 of the 2-ounce bowls, combine the baking soda and just enough water so it dissolves completely.

3. Fill the other 5 bowls with 1 solution each—the lemon juice, vinegar, milk, colorless window cleaner solution, and ammonia.

4. Using the eyedropper, add 1 drop of the turmeric indicator to each of the solutions in the small glass bowls. Pause for a second and then add 2 or 3 more. Watch carefully.

AWESOME CHEMISTRY EXPERIMENTS FOR KIDS

- 2 teaspoons powdered turmeric (Now Try This!)
- ½ cup baking soda (Now Try This!)
- An ice cube tray (Now Try This!)
- Lemon-lime soda (Now Try This!)

Observations: What happened to the color of the turmeric when it was mixed with the rubbing alcohol? What about when it was dropped into each of the other bowls?

The Hows and Whys: Turmeric contains a chemical compound that can change color. When it is combined with an acid, it remains yellow, but when it is added to a base (the chemical opposite of an acid), the atoms and bonds in the compound move around to make a new compound that is red.

Now Try This! Mix 2 teaspoons turmeric with ½ cup baking soda and a little water. Mix until it makes a paste. Spoon the mixture into an ice cube tray and freeze overnight. When frozen, drop the "turmeric ice cubes" into some colorless solutions like lemon-lime soda, distilled white vinegar, tap water, or distilled water.

STEAM CONNECTION: Acids and bases are measured on the **pH scale**. The pH scale usually has numbers from 0 to 14, in which a number less than 7 indicates an acid, and a number greater than 7 indicates a base. Seven is considered neutral. Indicators change color to help chemists identify a substance as an acid or as a base. The acid in your stomach that is used to break down food has a low pH, usually around 1-3.

ACID TESTING

MATERIALS

- Measuring spoons
- Measuring cups
- Small bowls
- ⅜ teaspoon washing soda, divided (note that this is different from baking soda)
- 3 cups water, divided
- Phenolphthalein solution (buy online)
- Eyedroppers
- Distilled white vinegar
- A spoon
- Lemon juice
- Lemon-lime soda
- Citric acid (Now Try This!)

 Which household acids are the most acidic?

 Caution: Handle phenolphthalein with goggles, gloves, and adult supervision.

THE STEPS

1. In a small bowl, mix ⅛ teaspoon of washing soda into 1 cup of water. Stir well.

2. Using an eyedropper, add 2 or 3 drops of phenolphthalein to the washing soda solution.

3. Using another eyedropper, start adding vinegar to the washing soda solution, 1 drop at a time. After each drop, stir using a spoon. Carefully count the number of drops you add and keep watching the solution. Continue adding the vinegar drop by drop until you notice a change.

4. Repeat steps 1 through 3 but replacing the vinegar in step 3 with lemon juice.

5. Repeat steps 1 through 3 a second time with lemon-lime soda.

Observations: What do you notice when you add the phenolphthalein to the washing soda in step 2? Which acid (the vinegar, lemon juice, or lemon-lime soda) used the fewest drops to make the change in step 3?

The Hows and Whys: The acids in vinegar, lemon juice, and lemon-lime soda will react to remove the base in the washing soda, allowing the indicator to show a different color.

Now Try This! Make 3 different solutions of citric acid by dissolving ¼, ½, and 1 teaspoon citric acid in 1 cup water each in 3 separate bowls. Repeat the experiment using these acid solutions in place of the vinegar.

STEAM CONNECTION: Some acids found in the home like the one found in vinegar are weak and relatively safe—so safe that you can actually eat and drink them in the form salad dressings, red wine vinegar, rice vinegar, and balsamic vinegar. Others are strong, like muriatic used for cleaning stonework, and are very dangerous.

ANTACID RAINBOW

DIFFICULTY: EASY

TIME: 20 MINUTES

MESS-O-METER: MINOR MESS

MATERIALS

- Measuring cups
- 5 mL liquid antacid (milk of magnesia, such as Mylanta)
- A large glass
- 40 mL (8 medicine cups) distilled water
- 5-10 ice cubes
- Universal indicator (order online)
- A spoon
- Distilled white vinegar
- Red cabbage (Now Try This!)

 How does an antacid help your upset stomach?

 Caution: Universal indicator needs to be handled with goggles, gloves, and adult supervision.

THE STEPS

1. Pour the liquid antacid into the large glass. You can use one of the medicine cups that usually comes with the bottle to measure. Add the distilled water. Add the ice cubes and stir well. (Be sure to use distilled water, since tap water may contain extra chemicals that could ruin the experiment!)

2. Add 10 drops of universal indicator until a very obvious color is displayed.

3. While stirring, add about ¼ cup of white vinegar. Watch the solution carefully as you stir.

4. After 2 minutes and observing a color change, add some more vinegar, once again with plenty of stirring.

Observations: Carefully make a note of all of the color changes that you see, especially as they change over time.

The Hows and Whys: Universal indicator is a chemical that changes color depending on the level of acidity present. In low acidity, there will be one color, in high acidity another. The antacid slowly reacts with the acidic vinegar, neutralizing it, and the indicator shows a range of colors as the reaction happens.

Now Try This! Instead of buying universal indicator, make your own indicator by slicing one-quarter of a red cabbage and boiling it in water. Collect the concentrated cabbage juice from the pot to use as indicator.

STEAM CONNECTION: Antacid stands for "anti-acid." Antacids are used to react with extra stomach acid when your tummy is a little grumbly! Antacids are part of a group of chemicals called bases that are the chemical opposites of acids. When a base reacts with an acid in this way, it is called a **neutralization** reaction. Like acids, bases can be dangerous. Many drain cleaners are strong bases and can be corrosive.

HIDDEN LAYERS

MATERIALS

- Sandpaper
- An empty soda can
- A long, thin rod, such as a knitting needle
- Drain cleaner
- A tall glass container

 What does the inside of a soda can look like?

 Caution: Drain cleaner is very destructive and should be handled with gloves, goggles, and adult supervision. Complete the activity outside or in a well-ventilated area.

THE STEPS

1. Using the sandpaper, remove all of the design from the can to leave a shiny metal surface.

2. Thread the knitting needle through the ring pull of the open can, so that the can hangs below the needle. Open the can, and adjust the ring pull so that the knitting needle can pass through it and suspend the can underneath.

3. Pour drain cleaner into the tall glass container.

4. Carefully lower the can into the drain cleaner so that the knitting needle sits on the rim of the glass container but the can is almost completely submerged. Leave the can in the drain cleaner for 1 hour.

5. Carefully remove the can from the drain cleaner using the knitting needle.

Observations: Check on the can several times during the experiment and see if you notice any changes taking place.

The Hows and Whys: Most drain cleaners contain a chemical called sodium hydroxide that can react with and dissolve a thin, aluminum can. The can is lined with a plastic layer to prevent any metallic taste from getting into the drink. It also protects the metal can from being corroded by the (often acidic) drink. The plastic does not react with the sodium hydroxide.

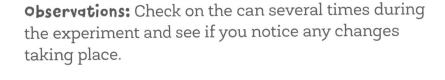

Now Try This! Repeat the experiment, but this time, do not use the sandpaper to remove the design. Does the experiment still work? Why or why not? What differences do you notice?

STEAM CONNECTION: Strong bases like the sodium hydroxide in drain cleaner are just as corrosive as strong acids, like muriatic acid, that are used to clean concrete and swimming pools. Bases are the chemical opposite of acids. They react with acids to produce water. Like acids, they can react with metals to dissolve them. Sodium hydroxide, when used carefully, can be used to clean aluminum metal by removing a thin layer of the metal.

ORANGE PEEL, POP, POOF!

DIFFICULTY: EASY

TIME: 20 MINUTES

MESS-O-METER: MINOR MESS

MATERIALS

- A natural latex balloon (such as a water balloon)
- An orange
- A knife
- A candle
- A multi-purpose lighter

 Are there chemicals in an orange?

 Cautions: Burning candles are hot and can burn you. Ask an adult for help with this one. Sharp knives should only be handled with adult supervision.

THE STEPS

1. Blow up a latex balloon and tie it off.

2. Peel the orange and cut the whole peel into 4 separate pieces.

3. Hold 1 of the pieces of peel a few centimeters above the balloon, and fold and squeeze the peel in your fingers. Brace yourself!

4. For the second half of the experiment, have an adult light a candle and turn out the lights.

5. Hold another piece of orange peel a few centimeters to the side of the flame, and fold and squeeze the peel in your fingers.

Observations: What do you notice when you squeeze the orange peel over the balloon? What about when you hold it over the candle? Do you see anything close to the surface of the peel itself?

The Hows and Whys: Squeezing the peel releases a naturally occurring chemical compound in the orange. It dissolves the latex in the balloon, causing it to split open and pop. The same chemical is flammable, which is why you see the flame flash.

Now Try This! Using a cell phone, take a video of each of the reactions and slow them down as much as you can. The slow-motion video will be spectacular! Also, you can try the experiment with other citrus fruits like lemons, limes, or grapefruits.

STEAM CONNECTION: The chemical compound in the orange peel is called limonene. Squeezing the peel releases a very fine spray of it into the air. Both the limonene and the latex rubber from the balloon are non-polar molecules. Chemists often say, "like dissolves like," and in this case, this means one non-polar molecule will dissolve another non-polar molecule. Limonene is flammable, and it combusts (or burns) in the oxygen in the air. Water is the most common polar molecule that you know. That makes it really good at dissolving things that are also polar, like alcohols, to make solutions.

DISSOLVING PACKING PEANUTS

DIFFICULTY: EASY

TIME: 30 MINUTES

MESS-O-METER: MINOR MESS

MATERIALS

- 4 (6-ounce) water glasses or baby food jars
- 6 ounces acetone
- 6 ounces water
- 2 Styrofoam packing peanuts
- 2 cornstarch packing peanuts
- A metal spoon

Can liquids dissolve solids?

Caution: Acetone should be handled with care and adult supervision in a well-ventilated room.

THE STEPS

1. Fill 2 of the 4 small glasses halfway with the acetone. Fill the other 2 glasses halfway with the water.

2. Place 1 Styrofoam packing peanut into a glass containing acetone and the other into a glass containing water.

3. Place 1 cornstarch packing peanut into a glass containing acetone and the other into a glass containing water.

4. Using the metal spoon, gently stir the glasses, observing the packing peanuts carefully over a period of about 15 minutes.

Observations: Look closely to see if either type of packing peanut floats in either liquid.

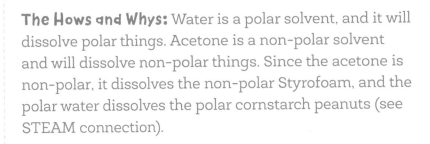

The Hows and Whys: Water is a polar solvent, and it will dissolve polar things. Acetone is a non-polar solvent and will dissolve non-polar things. Since the acetone is non-polar, it dissolves the non-polar Styrofoam, and the polar water dissolves the polar cornstarch peanuts (see STEAM connection).

Now Try This! Acetone will dissolve various types of plastic. Experiment by placing small pieces of plastic in acetone overnight and checking them in the morning.

STEAM CONNECTION: The phrase "like dissolves like" applies here. It is often used to describe the behavior of solids in liquids. A solid that has tiny positive and negative charges as part of its structure is called polar. Liquids can also be polar. When the positive and negative charges on a polar solvent and polar solid are attracted to one another, the solvent surrounds the solid and dissolves it. Non-polar solvents will surround non-polar solids and dissolve them. Common table salt has positive and negative particles called ions that polar water can surround, meaning that water can dissolve salt very easily. Acetone is a common chemical in the home, as it is used as nail polish remover.

ORANGE CANDLE

DIFFICULTY: MEDIUM
TIME: 30 MINUTES
MESS-O-METER: MINOR MESS

MATERIALS

- Measuring spoons
- A small orange, such as a tangerine or a mandarin
- A small paring knife
- A small plate
- 3 tablespoons olive oil
- A multi-purpose lighter

 Can cooking oils be used as fuel for candles?

 Caution: An open flame can burn. Make sure to get an adult to help with this one. Sharp knives should only be handled with adult supervision.

THE STEPS

1. Ask an adult to cut into the peel all the way around the middle of the orange using a paring knife. Cut horizontally around the orange, so that all that you cut is the peel and not the flesh of the orange itself.

2. Carefully separate the 2 halves of the peel from the whole orange by gently twisting and pulling. The bottom half of the peel should separate with the central, white pith still attached and standing upright. You might have to remove the orange slices, being careful to leave the middle stem portion intact.

3. Stand the orange peel on the plate and pour the olive oil over the pith wick and into the orange peel. Make sure the wick gets really soaked by the olive oil.

4. Using the multi-purpose lighter, light the wick of your orange candle. You may need to be patient here and hold the lighter close to the wick for a little while.

Observations: Watch and listen to the burning olive oil. Describe what you see and hear.

The Hows and Whys: Olive oil is flammable, but it is almost impossible to set fire to a large bowl of it with a lighter. But if it's concentrated in the orange wick, it's much easier to set fire to it. Just like it's a lot easier to heat up a small amount of water than a large amount of water, when there's only a tiny amount of oil present, it's easier to heat it up to get it to light.

Now Try This! Try the candle using other types of kitchen oils, such as canola oil, coconut oil, avocado oil, or sesame oil. Which ones light most easily and burn the best?

STEAM CONNECTION: When cooking, it's best to keep the oil that you are using below what is called the smoke point. The smoke point is the temperature at which the oil stops shimmering and starts to smoke. When this happens, the oil is beginning to break down into other chemicals and can produce a bitter or burned taste. Yuk!

SELF-EXTINGUISHING CANDLE

DIFFICULTY: EASY

TIME: 10 MINUTES

MESS-O-METER: MINOR MESS

MATERIALS

- A candle
- A shallow bowl or a plate that can hold liquid
- Water
- Food coloring
- A Mason jar
- A hydrogen peroxide contact lens cleaning case (such as Clear Care) (Now Try This!)

 What is needed for a candle to burn?

Caution: Lit candles are hot and can burn you. Ask an adult for help with this one.

THE STEPS

1. Place the candle in the center of the bowl.

2. Pour water into the bowl so that it reaches about halfway up the candle and add a few drops of food coloring to the water.

3. Light the candle.

4. Place the Mason jar over the candle and onto the bowl and watch carefully.

Observations: Watch the candle and the level of the water in the jar as the candle burns. What happens?

The Hows and Whys: The burning candle uses up all of the oxygen in the air inside of the Mason jar, and when the oxygen is all used up, the candle can no longer burn. As the oxygen inside the jar is used up, the pressure inside the jar drops because the candle flame uses up all the gases. The **atmospheric pressure** (outside of the jar) is greater than the pressure inside the jar, and the difference in pressure forces the water up into the jar. When a pressure difference between liquids or gases exists, the liquid or gas will always pass from the high-pressure area to the low-pressure area.

Now Try This! Pour some 6 percent hydrogen peroxide into a hydrogen peroxide contact lens cleaning case, and place the lid on top of the case, but don't screw it on. Place the case next to the candle from the original step 1 and repeat the experiment with the candle and the contact lens case under the Mason jar. See what happens to the candle this time.

STEAM CONNECTION: Combustion is a reaction between a fuel and oxygen. The source of oxygen is usually just the air around us, which is made up of 21 percent oxygen (the remainder is mostly nitrogen). Oxygen is part of the **fire triangle**, and it is necessary for anything to burn. Remove any one of the pieces of the triangle, and fire cannot be created. A combustion reaction between oxygen and gasoline is the chemical reaction that provides the energy for a car engine to work. In fact, a car engine is called an *internal combustion engine*.

RELIGHTING A CANDLE

DIFFICULTY: EASY

TIME: 10 MINUTES

MESS-O-METER: MINOR MESS

MATERIALS

- A candle
- A multi-purpose lighter

 What parts of a candle burn? The wick or something else?

Caution: Lit candles are hot and can burn you. Ask an adult for help with this one.

THE STEPS

1. In a room with no drafts, light the candle, and allow it to burn for a minute.

2. Have an adult ignite the lighter using the trigger and holding it in the on position.

3. Blow out the candle and follow the smoke trail very carefully with your eyes.

4. Immediately bring the lit lighter to the end of the smoke trail, a few centimeters above the wick, and watch as the candle relights from a distance!

Observations: When the candle is burning, what does the smoke trail look like?

The Hows and Whys: Candle wax melts into liquid, which then evaporates into vapor, which is a gas. The smoke trail that emerges when the candle is extinguished shows where the vaporized candle wax is traveling through the air. It's the vaporized wax that is flammable, so placing the lighter in the smoke trail will relight the vapor. That vapor then traces a path back down to the candle wick, relighting the candle.

Now Try This! Repeat the experiment several times. See how far away from the wick you get and still relight the candle. Start about 6 inches away from the top of the candle and move closer if that doesn't work.

STEAM CONNECTION: It's not the wick that is burning in a candle, rather it's the vaporized candle wax. All fires need fuel, oxygen, and a heat source (the fire triangle) to get the combustion reaction going, and here the fuel is the wax vapor. The heat source is the lighter and the oxygen comes from the air around the wick. One way to stop a fire burning is to starve it of oxygen. That's how fire blankets work.

BATTERY FIRE!

DIFFICULTY: EASY

TIME: 20 MINUTES

MESS-O-METER: MAJOR MESS

MATERIALS

- Fine steel wool
- A baking sheet
- Goggles
- Oven mitts
- A 9V battery
- Scissors
- Aluminum foil
- AA battery
- Other battery sizes (such as AAA, etc.) (Now Try This!)

 How do electrical fuses work?

 Cautions: This one starts an actual fire, so adult supervision is required. Be very careful, and dispose of the batteries properly. Keep the flames and their sparks away from flammable objects.

THE STEPS

1. Loosen the fibers of a tennis ball–size wad of steel wool by lightly pulling on it.

2. Spread the steel wool out onto the baking sheet. It does not need to cover the entire baking sheet.

3. Have an adult wearing goggles and oven mitts pick up the 9V battery and touch the terminals to the steel wool and watch what happens from a safe distance.

4. For the second part of the experiment, cut a piece of aluminum foil about 10 cm long and 1 cm wide.

5. In the middle of the foil, cut a deep V-shape so that the foil stays in one piece, but so that the foil width is made very small.

6. Have an adult wearing the goggles and oven mitts touch the ends of the foil to opposite ends of the AA battery, and watch what happens from a safe distance.

Observations: Watch the thin metal pieces in each part of the experiment. Which one catches fire more easily?

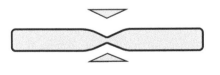

The Hows and Whys: The batteries convert chemical potential energy to electrical energy (see *Coin Battery* experiment, page 72). In each reaction, the metal (steel wool or aluminum foil) completes an electrical circuit with the battery. The electricity passes through the thin metal, producing lots of heat. Making the metal very thin means that it cannot absorb all of the energy, and it burns by reacting with oxygen in the air.

Now Try This! Experiment with different batteries (AAA, D, etc.) and different widths of aluminum foil. Which combinations work best?

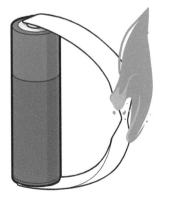

STEAM CONNECTION: These reactions are exactly how electrical fuses work. A fuse contains a thin piece of wire that completes the circuit. If there is a fault in the circuit and too much electricity passes, the fuse wire will burn out, and the circuit will be broken. This protects the circuit from being damaged.

PENNY CATALYST

DIFFICULTY: MEDIUM
TIME: 20 MINUTES
MESS-O-METER: MINOR MESS

MATERIALS

- Acetone
- A heat-resistant glass container, such as Pyrex
- A hand drill
- A pre-1982 penny or copper wire that has been twisted into a tight spiral
- Medium-gauge copper wire
- Tongs
- An open-flame heat source, such as blow-torch or gas stove top
- A knitting needle or other metal rod

How do you speed up a chemical reaction?

Cautions: This experiment must be done with an adult's help in a well-ventilated space. Always keep highly flammable acetone away from the open flame.

THE STEPS

1. Pour enough acetone into the heat-resistant container to get a depth of about 3 or 4 cm.

2. Have an adult drill a hole through a pre-1982 penny. Thread a length of wire through the hole in the penny, or through the spiraled wire, and twist into a tie to make a loop. The loop should be just long enough to suspend the penny about 2-3 cm *above* the surface of the acetone.

3. Have an adult hold the copper loop using the tongs, and heat the penny in the open flame until it glows red.

4. Carefully thread the knitting needle through the copper wire loop and place the knitting needle on the top of the heat-resistant container so that the penny is suspended 2-3 cm above the surface of the acetone (just like you measured for).

5. Lift the penny away from the acetone for about 10 seconds, then hold it over the acetone once more.

Observations: Keep a close eye on the penny as it is heated, when it is suspended over the acetone, when you lift it away from the acetone, and when you return it.

The Hows and Whys: Acetone vapors are flammable, but without the copper **catalyst** they will not react with oxygen in the air. The hot penny provides a surface for the reaction between acetone and oxygen to take place.

Now Try This! Repeat the experiment, but this time, just before you suspend the penny over the acetone for the first time, turn out the lights!

STEAM CONNECTION: A reaction where a fuel, like acetone, is burned is called a combustion reaction. A combustion reaction occurs between the fuel and oxygen in the air. Catalysts are substances that make chemical reactions go faster. A substance that is used to slow down a reaction is called an **inhibitor**. The production of a very important chemical called ammonia, NH_3, depends on a catalyst. Ammonia is crucial to the world because it is used in the manufacture of fertilizers. Ammonia is produced in a reaction between hydrogen and nitrogen gas that is catalyzed by iron metal.

DOUGHY CIRCUITS

MATERIALS

- ➔ A wooden spoon
- ➔ 4 AA batteries and a battery holder
- ➔ An LED light

FOR THE CONDUCTING DOUGH:

- ➔ Measuring cups
- ➔ Measuring spoons
- ➔ A saucepan
- ➔ 1 cup tap water
- ➔ 1 cup flour, plus more as needed
- ➔ ¼ cup salt
- ➔ 2 tablespoons cream of tartar
- ➔ 1 tablespoon vegetable oil
- ➔ Blue food coloring

? Why do the lights come on when the switch is flipped?

! Caution: **You'll be using the stove, so you'll need an adult's help.**

THE STEPS

1. **To make the conducting dough:** In the saucepan, mix together the water, flour, salt, cream of tartar, vegetable oil, and a few drops of blue food coloring. Constantly stir it over medium heat. When a tennis ball–size blob forms, turn off the heat.

2. Let the conducting dough cool, and if necessary, roll it in a little more flour to make it less sticky. Split the dough into 2 equal-size lumps.

3. **To make the non-conducting dough:** In the large bowl, mix together the flour, sugar, vegetable oil, and a few drops of red food coloring. Slowly add the distilled water and mix constantly until a non-sticky dough forms. Adjust the water and flour amounts to get a workable dough.

4. Assemble the circuit with 1 of the battery pack wires going into 1 lump of blue conducting dough and the other wire going into the other lump. Place the lump of red non-conducting dough snugly between the 2 conducting lumps. Place 1 wire of the LED into 1 blue conducting lump of dough, and the other wire into the other blue conducting lump of dough.

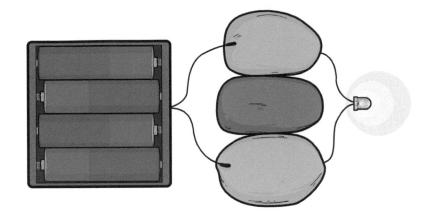

FOR THE NON-CONDUCTING DOUGH:

- ➔ Measuring cups
- ➔ Measuring spoons
- ➔ A large bowl
- ➔ 1 cup flour
- ➔ ½ cup sugar
- ➔ 2 tablespoons vegetable oil
- ➔ Red food coloring
- ➔ ½ cup distilled water

Observations: Try to connect the circuit without the non-conducting dough and see what happens.

The Hows and Whys: Electricity needs a free-moving charge carrier to flow. Charge carriers can be electrons (this is how metals conduct electricity) or particles with positive and negative charges called **ions**. The salt and the cream of tartar in the conducting dough have lots of these ions, making the dough a great conductor. We use the non-conducting dough to force the electricity to pass through the LED.

Now Try This! Do some research to find out if other household chemicals like baking soda or salt have ions and test them in new conducting doughs.

STEAM CONNECTION: All batteries have some kind of electrolyte (a conducting material) inside of them. Sometimes it can be a liquid, sometimes a paste, but the electrolyte contains ions that can flow through the battery and produce electricity.

COIN BATTERY

DIFFICULTY: MEDIUM
TIME: 45 MINUTES
MESS-O-METER: MINOR MESS

MATERIALS

- Measuring cups
- Measuring spoons
- A small bowl
- ¼ cup vinegar
- 1 tablespoon salt
- Scissors
- A kitchen paper towel
- 4 pennies
- 4 nickels
- Steel wool
- Aluminum foil
- An LED light
- Wires
- Voltmeter (optional)

 What makes a battery work?

 Cautions: **None**

THE STEPS

1. In the bowl, mix together the vinegar and salt.

2. Cut a kitchen paper towel into at least 4 (2-cm) squares.

3. Dip the kitchen towel squares into the vinegar and salt solution. The squares should be wet but not dripping.

4. Clean the pennies and nickels by rubbing them with the steel wool, then cleaning them in the vinegar and salt solution. Dry them thoroughly.

5. Cut a piece of aluminum foil 3 cm wide and 12 cm long. Fold it over twice lengthwise to make 3 layers and to make it 1 cm wide.

6. Lay the foil strip on the table, and at one end of the strip make a stack of 1 penny, 1 paper towel square, and 1 nickel. Repeat the stack in the exact same order 3 more times. Make sure that the paper towel squares are small enough to stay just between the coins and not stick out of the sides.

7. Connect the LED light by touching 1 of the wire connectors to the top nickel, and 1 of the connectors to the aluminum foil strip. If you have a voltmeter, you can also measure the voltage.

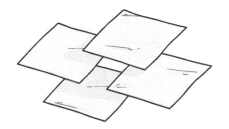

Observations: Make a note of what the coins look like when you've cleaned them and look at them again after the experiment is done.

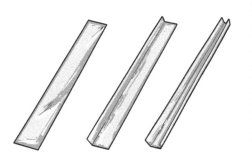

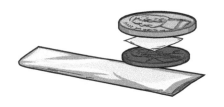

The Hows and Whys: You've made a small battery! Electrons that act as the charge carriers are passed from one metal to the other. When electrons flow, we have electricity! All batteries use chemical reactions called REDOX reactions. In REDOX reactions, two different substances (in this case, the two metals in the two different coins) have different levels of reactivity—one will lose electrons more easily than the other and one will gain electrons more easily. When one substance passes electrons to another substance and those electrons pass through a wire, we have electricity. After all of the electrons have been passed from one substance to the other, the battery dies. We can recharge a battery by sending the electrons back to their starting position, then have them passed once more.

Now Try This! Make the battery 2 or 3 times the size by using more coins and more paper towels in the same order as before. Try powering a small electric motor or a fan instead of the LED. If you use the voltmeter, pay attention to what happens to the voltage when you use more coins.

STEAM CONNECTION: Biochemistry scientists at MIT have been working on a project to build batteries from viruses.

BROWN APPLES

MATERIALS

- Measuring spoons
- Measuring cups
- A knife
- A large apple
- 1 tablespoon baking soda
- 4 ounces water (tap water is fine for this), divided
- A small bowl
- 4 ounces milk
- 4 ounces lemon juice
- 4 ounces vinegar
- 6 short glasses

 Why do apples get brown?

Caution: Sharp knives should only be handled with adult supervision.

THE STEPS

1. Have an adult cut the apple into 6 equal-size slices.

2. Make a baking soda solution by mixing the baking soda with 2 ounces of water in the bowl.

3. Pour the milk, lemon juice, vinegar, baking soda solution, and remaining 2 ounces of water into separate glasses. Make sure there's enough liquid in each glass to cover three-fourths of the apple slice. Leave the sixth glass empty.

4. Place an apple slice into each of the 5 glasses of liquids, ensuring that about one-quarter of each apple slice is exposed to the air. Put the remaining apple slice in the empty glass.

5. Allow the apples to brown over time, checking on them every hour for a total of 6 hours.

Observations: After each hour, make a note of the amount of browning and any different shades of color for all of the different liquids.

The Hows and Whys: The browning of apples is caused by a reaction between a chemical in the apples and oxygen in the air. Anything that can either prevent the compound in the apples coming into contact with oxygen, or that interferes with the reaction itself, will help slow down the browning process.

Now Try This! Try using distilled water instead of tap water in the experiment. Does that make a difference? Also try browning different fruits, such as pears.

STEAM CONNECTION: Cutting apples damages their cells, and through a combination of complicated chemical reactions involving naturally occurring compounds called polyphenol oxidase (PPO) and polyphenols, the pigment melanin is formed. Melanin makes things look brown. Melanin is found in your skin, and it gives your skin its color.

LIPTASTIC!

DIFFICULTY: EASY
TIME: 30 MINUTES
MESS-O-METER:
MEDIUM MESS

MATERIALS

- Measuring spoons
- A saucepan
- 2 tablespoons beeswax
- 2 tablespoons honey
- Vitamin E oil
- 2 tablespoons almond oil
- A spoon
- ½ teaspoon essential oil, such as peppermint
- A glass container with spout
- 3-ounce aluminum tins or lip balm tubes
- A funnel (optional)

 Why do we use lip balm to protect our lips?

Caution: You'll be using the stove, so you'll need an adult's help.

THE STEPS

1. In the saucepan, combine the beeswax, honey, a few drops of vitamin E oil, and the almond oil. Gently heat over low heat, stirring constantly, for a few minutes, or until melted. The mixture can burn quite easily, so it's important to keep the heat low while you stir constantly.

2. When the ingredients are completely smooth, stir in the essential oil, and continue to mix.

3. After a few minutes, the whole mixture will be ready to pour into the aluminum tins. Remove from the heat. Transfer it from the saucepan to a glass measuring cup or something glass with a spout. It's a lot easier to pour the liquid lip balm into tins than it is to pour into the tubes, but the tubes are more like the real thing. If you are using the tubes, use a funnel to help get the liquid into the tubes.

Observations: Watch the saucepan mixture carefully as you heat it. Do you see the beeswax and oil mixing well? Things that mix well are called *miscible*. Things that don't, like oil and water, are called *immiscible*.

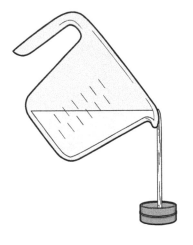

The Hows and Whys: In the winter, it's very easy for lips to become dry and cracked as they lose moisture. The lip balm provides a protective layer on the lips. The layer is called an *occlusive agent*. It traps the moisture that naturally occurs in the skin and protects it from the environment.

Now Try This! You can experiment with different oils. Instead of almond oil, you can use coconut oil. Each oil gives a slightly different feel (more creamy versus less creamy) and a slightly different taste to the balm. The same is true when you experiment with the essential oils. Good essential oils to try are classic peppermint, lemon, and lavender. You can also try adding other ingredients like cocoa or shea butter. Lots of experimenting will change the consistency (how hard or soft it is) of the balm, how it feels, how it smells, how it tastes, and how well it works!

STEAM CONNECTION: All lip balm recipes use oils and waxes. Oils and waxes are hydrophobic, meaning that they don't mix well with water. This helps keep the water in your lips. Oils and waxes are compounds made of various combinations of the elements carbon, hydrogen, and oxygen. Emollients like honey and oils help smooth the skin. Waxes are applied to the paint-work of cars to protect them from the weather.

MOO GLUE

MATERIALS

- Measuring cups
- Measuring spoons
- 1 cup skim milk
- A medium saucepan
- 1 tablespoon distilled white vinegar
- A wooden spoon
- A fine-mesh sieve
- ¼ cup water
- 1 tablespoon baking soda
- Pieces of paper or cardboard

 What is cottage cheese?

 Caution: You'll be using the stove, so you'll need an adult's help.

THE STEPS

1. Pour the skim milk into the saucepan.

2. Add the white vinegar to the milk and stir.

3. Heat the saucepan over medium heat, being careful not to burn the milk. Stir constantly using the wooden spoon.

4. When you see lumps in the milk, take the saucepan off the heat, but keep stirring.

5. Pour the milk through the fine-mesh sieve. You need the solid parts (the curds), but you can pour the liquid part (the whey) down the sink.

6. Return the curds to the saucepan and add the water and baking soda. Gently heat the mixture over medium heat, stirring gently constantly. When you see it start to bubble, take the saucepan off the heat, and let it cool.

7. You've now made glue, so use it to stick some pieces of paper or cardboard together.

Observations: Watch the milk carefully to see the curds separating. What do you notice when you add the baking soda?

The Hows and Whys: The **proteins** in milk are called caseins. Their reaction with the vinegar causes the milk to curdle and causes the proteins to separate out and to form into solids. The baking soda neutralizes any acid left over from the curdling reaction. Caseins are naturally sticky substances that were actually used as glues in aircraft manufacturing until the early part of the 19th century.

Now Try This! Try using different types of milk, including whole milk, soy milk, almond milk, or other nut milks to see which one makes the stickiest glue!

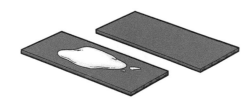

STEAM CONNECTION: Proteins are very important chemicals. They help build, maintain, and replace the body's tissues that make up muscles and organs. Foods high in protein are important for growth. One of those foods is cottage cheese, and that's what you just made! In cottage cheese–making, rennet, a special type of enzyme from the stomachs of cows, is typically used instead of vinegar.

BATH BOMBS

DIFFICULTY: EASY
TIME: 30 MINUTES TO
MAKE, BUT 2 DAYS FOR
THE BOMBS TO DRY OUT
AND WORK
MESS-O-METER:
MEDIUM MESS

MATERIALS

- Measuring cups
- Measuring spoons
- Large and small mixing bowls
- 3 cups baking soda
- 1 cup Epsom salts
- 1 cup citric acid
- 1 teaspoon water
- 1 tablespoon olive oil
- 3 or 4 drops food coloring
- A whisk or wooden spoon
- A mold (optional, but silicone baking tins work great)

 What happens when an acid reacts with a base?

 Cautions: None

THE STEPS

1. In a large mixing bowl, mix together the baking soda, Epsom salts, and citric acid.

2. In a small mixing bowl, mix together the water, olive oil, and food coloring.

3. Slowly and gradually, add the wet ingredients to the dry ingredients, and mix really well. Keep mixing until everything is evenly combined and the color is even throughout the mixture.

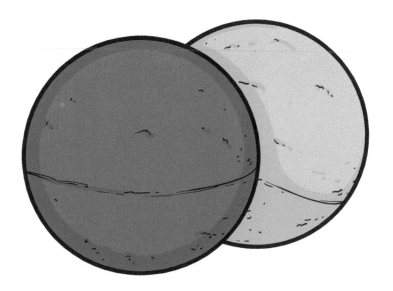

4. Using your hands or a mold, shape the mixture into bath bombs. If you're using your hands, aim for the size of a tennis ball.

5. You can use the bath bombs immediately if you'd like, but for best results, allow them to dry for 1-2 days, or until they are completely dry.

Observations: Watch carefully as you add the wet ingredients to the dry to see the start of the reaction.

The Hows and Whys: The citric acid will react with the baking soda to produce carbon dioxide gas. That's the fizz that you see. The dry ingredients will not react together until they go **in solution** with the water in the bath.

Now Try This! Experiment with the amounts of the dry ingredients to see if you can make even fizzier bath bombs by adding more citric acid. Also, add a few drops of some essential oils in step 2 to make the bath bombs smell great!

STEAM CONNECTION: A similar reaction that happens in this experiment takes place when an upset stomach is treated with indigestion tablets, like Tums.

SPARKLING CANDIES

DIFFICULTY: EASY
TIME: 10 MINUTES
MESS-O-METER: MINOR MESS

MATERIALS

- Wintergreen mints
- A heavy object that can be used to crush things (such as a pestle or a hammer)

 What happens when I crush hard candies?

Cautions: Ask an adult for help to use a hammer.

THE STEPS

1. Place several wintergreen mints on a hard surface.

2. Make the room as dark as possible. Try doing this at night, with all the lights in the house off and the curtains or blinds closed.

3. Have an adult help you use the hammer to crush the mints.

Observations: As the candies are being crushed, watch carefully. You can even use a cell phone to video the action!

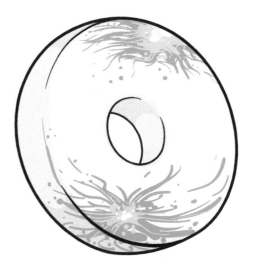

The Hows and Whys: When the sugar is crushed, the crystal structure is broken. When that happens, the electrons in the crystal structure jump around. When the electrons come into contact with the air, they ionize it, causing the flashes of light. It's a bit like tiny lightning bolts being formed in the mints! The creation of light by physically breaking or pulling apart a structure in this way is called *triboluminescence*.

Now Try This! Try crunching down a wintergreen mint in your mouth in a completely dark bathroom in front of a mirror. Probably not an experiment that your dentist would approve of, but still fun!

STEAM CONNECTION: Scientists don't completely understand triboluminescence, but they understand chemiluminescence (a different but similar phenomenon where light is emitted in a chemical reaction). In chemiluminescence, electrons move around inside atoms. When they move, they must gain energy. Electrons at higher energy levels are unstable and will eventually come down to a more stable, lower-energy position. Imagine a marble rolling around in a saucer. It will always come to rest at the bottom of the saucer in a low-energy, stable position. When electrons fall back down to a lower energy state, they give off their extra energy in the form of light. That's chemiluminescence! Glow sticks are a great example of chemiluminescence in action!

SECRET MESSAGES

DIFFICULTY: EASY

TIME: 30 MINUTES

MESS-O-METER:
MEDIUM MESS

MATERIALS

- Cotton swabs
- Phenolphthalein solution
- White paper
- Window cleaner in a spray bottle
- Measuring spoons (Now Try This!)
- Measuring cups (Now Try This!)
- 1 teaspoon baking soda (Now Try This!)
- 1 cup water (Now Try This!)
- Grape juice (Now Try This!)

 Why do some things have color?

! **Cautions:** Handle the phenolphthalein and window cleaner carefully.

THE STEPS

1. Dip a cotton swab into the phenolphthalein solution to get it wet, but not dripping. This will be your "pen."

2. On a piece of plain white paper, write a secret message using the cotton swab.

3. Set the paper aside, and allow it to dry completely.

4. Once the message has completely dried, spray the window cleaner onto the dry paper.

Observations: Watch your secret message appear before your very eyes!

The Hows and Whys: Phenolphthalein is an acid-base indicator that turns pink in **basic** solutions yet is colorless in acids. The window cleaner is a **dilute** solution of ammonia, and ammonia is a weak base. Acid and base indicators are very common in nature. Many naturally occurring chemicals are different colors depending on the pH (level of acidity) that is present. Low pH is caused by acids that produce high levels of hydrogen ions (H^+); bases are caused by very low levels of hydrogen ions.

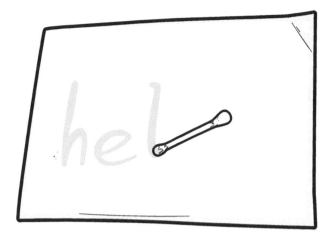

Now Try This! Instead of the phenolphthalein, make your invisible ink with a solution made from 1 teaspoon baking soda dissolved in 1 cup water. Use the cotton swab the same way and allow the message to dry once more. This time use grape juice to reveal the message (frozen concentrated grape juice is best).

STEAM CONNECTION: pH is an important concept in biology. Many of the chemical reactions in your body are dependent upon pH, and controlling it is important in making sure that your body functions correctly. pH is also important in gardening. One plant that is famous for changing color according to the pH of the soil is the hydrangea. Hydrangeas are blue in acidic soil, and pink in basic soil, the exact opposite of the colors we see with the most common chemistry lab indicator, litmus. For more about pH, try the *Spicy Indicators* experiment (page 48).

POLY SQUISHY!

DIFFICULTY: EASY
TIME: 30 MINUTES
MESS-O-METER:
MEDIUM MESS

MATERIALS

- Measuring spoons
- A spoon
- 1 teaspoon white glue (such as Elmer's)
- Water
- 2 small plastic cups
- Green food coloring (optional)
- 1 teaspoon powdered laundry detergent (such as Tide)
- Kitchen towels
- Liquid starch (Now Try This!)

 How do you make slime?

Cautions: None

THE STEPS

1. Mix the glue with 1 teaspoon of water into a small cup. Add a couple of drops of green food coloring for extra fun. Mix it up well.

2. Put the laundry detergent into the other small cup and add 1 tablespoon of water. Mix well.

3. Constantly stir the glue solution, and slowly add the laundry detergent solution until a blob forms in the cup. Note that it may not require all of the laundry solution.

4. Pat the blob dry between several kitchen towels.

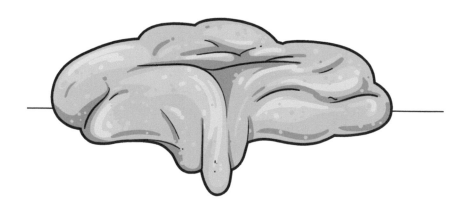

Observations: Make a careful note of what the glue looks and feels like before and after the addition of the laundry detergent.

The Hows and Whys: The **polymer chains** that are present in the glue can slide past one another easily. When the laundry detergent is added, it links those long polymer chains together. This is called *cross-linking of polymers.* Linking the chains together changes the consistency and feel of the polymer chains dramatically.

Now Try This! Put 1 teaspoon glue into a small cup as before but, this time, add liquid starch. The starch has a different chemical than the laundry detergent and joins the polymer chains in the glue in a completely different way. How can you tell that it is different than with the laundry detergent?

STEAM CONNECTION: Proteins, that is, the chemicals used for building muscles and tissues in the body, are polymers. They are made from amino acid building blocks that join together to create the long chain protein. Foods like beef, eggs, almonds, and chicken are all high in protein.

SHERBET

DIFFICULTY: EASY
TIME: 15 MINUTES
MESS-O-METER:
MEDIUM MESS

MATERIALS

- Measuring cups
- 1 cup citric acid
- 1 cup baking soda
- 5 cups confectioners' sugar
- 1 cup gelatin powder (such as Jell-O)
- A large bowl
- A mixing spoon

 What makes sherbet fizzy?

 Cautions: None

THE STEPS

1. Pour the citric acid, baking soda, confectioner's sugar, and gelatin powder into the large bowl.

2. Using a dry spoon, mix together the dry ingredients. It is very important to keep the mixture dry until it reaches your mouth.

3. Eat and enjoy!

Observations: What does it feel like in your mouth? Try adding some water to part of the sherbet mixture instead of eating it. Then you can see what's going on in your mouth!

The Hows and Whys: The reaction between the baking soda and the citric acid releases carbon dioxide gas that makes the fizziness in your mouth. The reaction between the solid citric acid and the solid baking soda is slow until it hits the moisture in your mouth.

Now Try This! See if you can change the fizziness of the sherbet by adjusting the recipe. The citric acid and the baking soda are the key ingredients for fizz! You can also adjust the sourness (acid) and the sweetness (sugar) to your own taste.

STEAM CONNECTION: Many reactions between solids are slow. When reactions are carried out in solution (usually in water) or when the chemicals are liquids or gases, the reaction can happen more quickly. In this experiment, the reaction doesn't start properly until the saliva in your mouth makes a solution with the solid ingredients. Rusting is an example of a really slow chemical reaction that takes many years, but an explosion is a reaction that can happen within just fractions of a second.

BUNCH OF BUBBLES

DIFFICULTY: EASY
TIME: 30 MINUTES
MESS-O-METER:
MEDIUM MESS

MATERIALS

- Measuring spoons
- 4 (4-ounce) plastic cups
- Distilled water
- 2 teaspoons salt
- 2 teaspoons Epsom salts
- 2 teaspoons plaster
  of paris
- Straws
- Baking soda
  (Now Try This!)
- Sugar (Now Try This!)

 Can water be slimy?

 Cautions: None

THE STEPS

1. Fill each of the plastic cups halfway with distilled water.

2. Put the salt in 1 of the cups, the Epsom salts in a second, and the plaster of paris in a third. The fourth cup should remain as plain water.

3. Stir all of the cups well. Try to dissolve as much of the solid as possible. The plaster of paris will not dissolve completely, but that's okay.

4. Using the straws, being careful not to inhale any of the mixture, blow air into each of the cups to make bubbles.

Observations: Pay attention to the amount of bubbles that you can make in each cup. Which one is easiest to make bubbles in?

The Hows and Whys: Water can be described as "hard" or "soft." Calcium and magnesium ions cause hardness in water. Epsom salts contain magnesium ions and plaster of paris contains calcium ions. Hard water makes it difficult to get soap to lather.

Now Try This! Try adding different solids, such as baking soda or sugar, to the water, and see if that makes a difference in the amount of bubbles that you can produce.

STEAM CONNECTION: Calcium ions form an insoluble compound with soap called calcium stearate. This is sometimes called soap scum. Soap scum prevents soft, soapy lather. It can also leave a nasty ring in the bathtub. Hard water is not only a problem because it's difficult to make a lather with or leaves things dirty, but also because it causes the buildup of solid magnesium and calcium compounds in pipes and water heaters. Those solids can cause the water heater to run inefficiently, so it costs more money to heat the water.

HEALTHY SALT

MATERIALS

- Measuring spoons
- Measuring cups
- Small bowls
- ½ teaspoon liquid laundry starch (such as Linit), divided
- 3½ cups distilled water, divided
- 5% tincture of iodine
- ¼ cup each of at least 3 different types of salt (for example, kosher salt, table salt, non-iodized salt, etc.)
- 3 tablespoons distilled white vinegar, divided
- 3 tablespoons 3% hydrogen peroxide, divided

 Which types of common salt have the most iodine?

 Cautions: None

THE STEPS

1. In a small bowl, combine the liquid laundry starch and ½ cup of distilled water. Add 2 or 3 drops of tincture of iodine.

2. In a separate bowl, dissolve ¼ cup of your first type of salt into 1 cup of distilled water. Not all of the salt will dissolve, but that's okay.

3. To the salt solution, add 1 tablespoon of vinegar, 1 tablespoon of hydrogen peroxide, and ½ teaspoon of starch-iodine solution. Stir the mixture for a few minutes.

4. Repeat the experiment (steps 2 and 3) with the other salt samples.

Observations: For each type of salt, notice how much time it takes for any colors to form and how dark those colors are.

The Hows and Whys: Iodine reacts when mixed with starch to create the blue-black color you see.

Now Try This! Repeat the experiment with even more salts, such as rock salt, pickling salt, and sea salt.

STEAM CONNECTION: Iodine is a necessary micro-nutrient for good health. It helps prevent a condition called goiter, where the thyroid gland in the neck becomes enlarged. A lack of iodine also causes problems with brain development. Many types of salt have iodine added to them to help avoid health problems that can happen if there is not enough iodine in someone's diet.

XYZ REACTION

MATERIALS

- Measuring cups
- Measuring spoons
- A spoon
- 2 (1000-mg) vitamin C tablets (not the chewable type)
- 3¾ cups distilled water, divided
- A funnel
- Coffee filters
- 2 glasses
- 5 teaspoons 5% tincture of iodine
- Removable tape
- A pen
- Saucepans
- ½ teaspoon cornstarch
- A source of heat (stove or microwave)
- ½ cup 3% hydrogen peroxide
- A large clear glass container
- A stopwatch

 How fast can a vitamin dissolve?

 Caution: You'll be using the stove, so you'll need an adult's help.

THE STEPS

1. Crush both 1000-mg vitamin C tablets and dissolve them in about ¼ cup of distilled water.

2. Line the funnel with a coffee filter, and filter the vitamin C solution into a glass to remove all of the solid pieces. This creates Solution X.

3. Add the tincture of iodine to the glass with Solution X and stir until the brown color disappears completely. Add 2 cups of distilled water. Label the resulting solution "Solution Y" using a piece of tape and a pen.

4. In a saucepan, mix together the cornstarch and remaining 1½ cups of distilled water, and heat over medium-high heat until as much of the cornstarch as possible is dissolved. Remove from the heat. If using a microwave, heat the mixture in a microwave-safe bowl in 10-second increments, checking after each one. Filter this solution using the funnel and coffee filter method from step 2 into a new glass. Allow the solution to cool to room temperature, and once cool, add the hydrogen peroxide to the glass. Label this solution "Solution Z."

Solution X

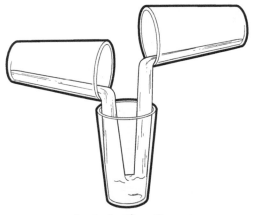

Mix Solution Y and Solution Z

Stir Solution Z

5. In the large clear glass container, mix 1 cup of Solution Y and 1 cup of Solution Z. Start the stopwatch right as you begin to stir. When you see a reaction, stop the stopwatch.

6. Warm 1 cup of Solution Y in a saucepan over medium heat (or microwave for about 1 minute) so that it is above room temperature, but not extremely hot or boiling. Do the same with 1 cup of Solution Z.

7. Repeat step 5, but this time use the warm solutions.

Observations: What do you notice about the speed of the reaction at different temperatures?

The Hows and Whys: There are three chemical reactions here. In Solution Y, vitamin C converts the tincture of iodine into something called iodide. When mixing Solutions Y and Z, hydrogen peroxide converts iodide back into iodine. Eventually all of the vitamin C gets used up and iodine reacts with the starch solution in another reaction to form a blue-black color.

Now Try This! Repeat the experiment by using either twice as much vitamin C in step 1 or twice as much tincture of iodine in step 3.

STEAM CONNECTION: Bread will rise more quickly in a warm place rather than a cool one and will bake more quickly at higher temperatures when compared to cooler ones.

KETCHUP GEYSER

DIFFICULTY: EASY
TIME: 20 MINUTES
MESS-O-METER: MAJOR MESS

MATERIALS

- A small shovel to dig a hole in the ground
- 1 (32-ounce) plastic ketchup bottle that is half-filled with ketchup
- A spoon
- Baking soda
- Goggles

 What is in ketchup?

 Cautions: Wear goggles, and don't point the ketchup bottle at anyone.

THE STEPS

1. Make sure you do this experiment outside. Dig a small hole in some dirt, big enough for the ketchup bottle to stand up in.

2. Unscrew the ketchup bottle cap completely.

3. Spoon the baking soda into the bottle, layering it carefully without shaking. Work as quickly as you can.

4. Once the bottle is about three-fourths full of ketchup and baking soda, quickly replace the cap.

5. Wearing goggles, stand close to the hole and start to shake the bottle, keeping 1 hand firmly over the cap.

6. After about 30 seconds of really strong shaking, place the bottle in the hole, and at arm's length, flip the cap open.

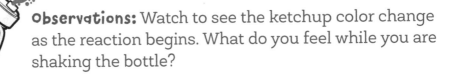

Observations: Watch to see the ketchup color change as the reaction begins. What do you feel while you are shaking the bottle?

The Hows and Whys: Ketchup has a lot of vinegar in it. Vinegar is a solution of ethanoic acid. Ethanoic acid will react with baking soda to produce carbon dioxide gas. When a gas is produced inside a sealed container, the pressure will start to build as the gas particles hit the wall of the container. Eventually the pressure becomes so great that the cap will be blown off, so that the gas can escape while bringing the contents of the bottle with it!

Now Try This! Try this experiment using different brands of ketchup. The acid content may vary, and you will get different results.

STEAM CONNECTION: Neutralization reactions like this one are important in the real world. For example, they can make soil less acidic so certain plants will grow better. Vegetables often grow well in soil that has a higher pH. Acids have a low pH, and calcium carbonate in the form of lime is added to make the soil less acidic. Beans, cabbages, peas, and leafy greens all benefit from a less-acidic soil.

Part III

PUTTING IT ALL TOGETHER

Chemistry is sometimes called "the central science."
Why? Because it's such an important part of so many other areas of science. Biology, geology, astronomy, physics, and biochemistry all have lots of chemistry in them. In fact, chemical reactions are everywhere!

In the modern world, we often call the subject areas all mixed together STEM (Science, Technology, Engineering, and Math). When we add Art, we sometimes use STEAM instead. Chemistry uses all of these subjects, even Art with the chemistry of colors or shapes of molecules. Either way, there's just no getting away from the chemistry that's all around you, every day.

Whether it was the explosions or the burning, the gases or the liquids, the hot or the cold, the colors that you saw or the fun that you had when you did the experiments, I hope that the chemistry in this book has excited and inspired you to investigate further and to find out more. Keep experimenting (safely!), and keep learning about the wonderful world of chemistry.

RESOURCES

Here's a list of some great chemistry books for kids.

Chemistry: Discover the Amazing Effect Chemistry Has on Every Part of Our Lives by Ann Newmark

The Elements by Adrian Dingle

How to Make a Universe with 92 Ingredients: An Electrifying Guide to the Elements by Adrian Dingle

The Cartoon Guide to Chemistry by Larry Gonick and Craig Criddle

The Kid's Book of the Elements: An Awesome Introduction to Every Known Atom in the Universe by Theodore Gray

The Periodic Table: Elements with Style! by Simon Basher and Adrian Dingle

Here's a list of some great places on the web to find out more about the wonderful world of chemistry. Have a parent help you access these.

Adrian Dingle's Chemistry Pages: AdrianDinglesChemistryPages.com

American Chemical Society's Kids' Resources: ACS.org/content/acs/en /education/outreach/kids-chemistry.html

Beautiful Chemistry, where you can find up-close videos of chemical reactions: BeautifulChemistry.net/reaction

Compound Interest, where you can find chemistry infographics galore: CompoundChem.com

Royal Society of Chemistry Kids' Resources: edu.RSC.org/resources/primary

GLOSSARY

ACID: A corrosive substance that is the chemical opposite of a base, producing hydrogen (H^+) ions in solution

ATMOSPHERIC PRESSURE: The pressure created by the gases in the atmosphere around us

ATOM: The basic building block of any element, made up of protons, neutrons, and electrons

BASE: A corrosive substance that is the chemical opposite of an acid, producing hydroxide (OH^-) ions in solution

BASIC: The property of a base

BOILING POINT: The temperature at which a substance changes from a liquid to a gas

CATALYST: A substance that speeds up a chemical reaction

COMBUSTION: Another word for burning, when a reaction with oxygen has occurred

COMPOUND: A substance made up of several chemical elements in fixed proportions

CONDENSATION: The change of state when a substance changes from a gas to a liquid

DENSITY: A measure of the ratio of the mass of a substance to its volume

DEPOSITION: The change of state when a substance changes from a gas directly to a solid, without passing through the liquid state

DILUTE: A solution where relatively little solute is dissolved into a relatively large amount of solvent

DISSOLVING: The process of taking a substance (a solute) and mixing it with a solvent (usually water) to make a solution

ELEMENT: A substance that cannot be chemically broken down to a simpler substance

ENZYME: A substance present in living organisms which acts as a catalyst for certain biochemical reactions

FIRE TRIANGLE: The elements needed for a fire to burn—oxygen, heat, and fuel

FREEZING POINT: The temperature at which a substance changes from a liquid to a solid

GAS: The state of matter in which the particles have the most energy and are most widely spaced

INDICATOR: A substance that changes colors depending on the pH of another substance

INHIBITOR: A substance that slows down a chemical reaction

INSOLUBLE: Not able to dissolve

IN SOLUTION: When a solute is dissolved in a solvent (usually water) to produce a solution that is a mixture of both the solute and the solvent, the solute is "in solution"

ION: A charged particle produced when an atom loses or gains electrons

LIQUID: The state of matter between a solid and a gas

LITMUS: A common acid-base indicator that is red in acid and blue in base

MASS: A measurable amount of matter in a substance

MATTER: Anything that has mass and volume

MOLECULE: A small group of atoms chemically bonded to one another

NEUTRALIZATION: The reaction between an acid and a base to produce salt and water

NON-POLAR: A substance with no charge

NUCLEATION SITE: A place where tiny gas particles can gather to form a mass large enough to see

PARTICLES: Small parts of substances

pH SCALE: A scale used to describe how acidic or basic a substance is. Less than 7 is acidic, more than 7 is basic, and 7 is neutral

POLAR: A substance with a charge

POLYMER CHAIN: Long chain molecules made up of repeat units called monomers

PROTEINS: Molecules that make up the structural tissue in the body

SOLUTION: Formed when one substance is dissolved in another to give a mixture of a solute and a solvent

SOLVENT: The substance that a solute dissolves in (e.g., water) to make a solution

SUBLIMATION: The change of state when a substance passes from solid directly to gas, without passing through the liquid state

SUBSTANCE: A particular type of matter

VOLUME: The amount of space that matter occupies

ACKNOWLEDGMENTS

Thank you to Julie and Phil for their ideas, inspiration, and support, and to all of the people who understand the particular kind of chemistry educator that I am.

Thank you to all at Callisto who worked on this project, in particular Matt, Laura, and Rebekah.

ABOUT THE AUTHOR

Adrian Dingle is a chemistry educator and author with more than 30 years of experience of teaching in the United States and the United Kingdom. He is the creator of the award-winning chemistry website AdrianDinglesChemistryPages.com.

He holds a BSc. (Hons.) Chemistry and a Postgraduate Certificate in Education (secondary chemistry), both from the University of Exeter in England.

He has also written *The Periodic Table: Elements with Style!*, *How to Make a Universe with 92 Ingredients*, and the DK Eyewitness: *The Elements* book and adapted Sam Kean's New York Times best seller *The Disappearing Spoon* for young readers.

He is the 2011 winner of the School Library Association of the UK's Information Book Award, and in 2012 he was honored with the *Wissenschaftsbüch des Jahres*, sponsored by the Austrian Federal Ministry of Education, Science, and Research. He also won the American Institute of Physics Science Communication Award for Children in 2014.

An Englishman, he lives, teaches, writes, and follows Leeds United FC MOT in Indiana, where he currently teaches at the Culver Academies.

Printed in the USA
CPSIA information can be obtained
at www.ICGtesting.com
CBHW081244200224
4500CB00005B/23